THE ANSWER IS ON THE INSIDE

By

Rosie Lee Rheaves

As Directed By The Divine Inspiration of The Holy Ghost

1663 LIBERTY DRIVE, SUITE 200
BLOOMINGTON, INDIANA 47403
(800) 839-8640
WWW.AUTHORHOUSE.COM

First published by AuthorHouse 04/27/05

ISBN: 1-4208-1468-0 (sc)

Library of Congress Control Number: 2004099149

Printed in the United States of America
Bloomington, Indiana

This book is printed on acid-free paper.

THE SPIRIT OF MAN IS THE CANDLE OF THE LORD,

SEARCHING ALL THE INWARD PARTS OF THE BELLY.

PROVERBS 20: 27

The Seed Planter Series: New Beginnings

Thou shalt also decree a thing, and it shall be established unto thee:
And the light shall shine upon thy ways.

Job 22:28

All Scripture quotations are taken from the King James Version

PERSONAL DEDICATIONS:

To my Heavenly Father, both Lord and Savior, Jesus Christ and His Anointing, You are my Jubilee!!! I stop to return and give thanks. My life is blessed because of your goodness and mercy. I will continue in the hope of my calling...and I surrender my life to worship the "Only One True Lover," of my soul.

To my Husband, Fletcher: Thank you for loving and choosing me. In our years together you have always demonstrated your commitment and without your support during this past year of writing this book it would have been most difficult. We are one in all things and united together...we conquer and win. I love you always!!!

To my Mother, Marie Randall, I'm proud of you and grateful for the sacrifices you made for me. I have a blessed and wonderful mother and appreciate what God is now doing in the lives of our family. May the Lord reward you with love, health and beautiful things!!!

To my Sisters: Stella Savage, Patricia Johnson, Lisa Randall and Teekewa Roundtree; thank you for sister love!!! You all have been a source of strength and endure the trials of life with great stories of your own to heal the brokenhearted. Continue in the Love of God and you all will surely be blessed!!!

To my Daughter, Monique Thompson and Son, Garrin Arnez Rheaves, know that I love you both and that I live this life to be a witness for the Lord. I am bound to teach you first the wisdom of God. Instructing you both to do the right things in life. Strive to climb higher in God and He will give you all the desires of your heart!!!

To Terri, Fletcher Jr., Johnnie Rheaves and Tanesha Johnson, your lovely spouses and beautiful children; you are also a part of me and I embrace the love that you have given me. I pray that the Lord will continue to empower our families as one and motivate us all to be a light of inspiration to others.

To Robin Karen Williams, You are a special and devoted friend. You will always be connected to me because of the Love of Jesus and nothing can separate our bond. I pray that you and the boys be blessed!!!

To Rayree Beasley: My technical support...thank you very much for everything. I'm so encouraged by your faith in me and the time and attention you provided to assist in making this dream to write my first book an accomplished reality. May you and your family have love, joy and happiness above measure!!!

TABLE OF CONTENTS

FORWARD ADDRESS:

"**. . .A**nd I shall not hesitate to obey the voice of The Lord My God. To keep his commandments and to do his will as He has ordained it to be so. For He (Jesus) has saved me and not another, He has called me by my name and He knows all about me...

I heard his supplications and answered, Yes Lord... Here Am I...I will obey!!!

This book is written by the direction and leading of the divine spirit of God of whom He alone deserves all honor and is most worthy of the praise that is due unto His most excellent name. There is no name so sweet, than the name of Jesus!!! For I have found that it is at the Name of Jesus that I am complete and He has made me free from sin and death; and live a spirit-filled life in submission to The Lord Jesus Christ and His Anointing. The very spirit of God shall have His way in me!!!

God appointed me to do this literary assignment. It was a calling from within my very being and existence. But God would have it to be so, and then it was a process and a coming forth from my heart and soul. My Lord Jesus tapped into the confines of my inner most parts and delivered a word...a thought...a message!!! God spoke and it was so....

And so I write of my past and present life to complete a true contrast that God is real and His power in us can save us from anything...even death!!! Whatever your situation, The Lord can solve it... journey with me through the pages of time in my life... to moments in your life and rediscover that if you have accepted Jesus, as your Lord and Savior; that for sure you can know that...THE ANSWER IS ON THE INSIDE... for whatever circumstances you are now facing.

I invite you to believe...trust God and obey His Word. If you are not saved or a follower of Christ, which is a Christian; you can be!!! Believe that Calvary's Cross was for you, God shed innocent blood ...His precious soul saving blood that gives us righteous freedom to be adoptive into the family of God, the right to sit in heavenly places; the right to have all our sins remitted, removed and forever forgotten...we are royalty dressed in God's righteousness...we have eternal life...now...we don't have to wait!! It is a blessing to know He is with us and will keep his promise. He is the Promise Keeper!! Attend your local church in your area and learn so much more about Jesus...Find the Bible teaching and believing, Holy Ghost filled, tongue talking church; that's not afraid to let God be God, where He is the Head of the Church...seek God earnestly for your place of fellowship!!

God will go before you and prepare the way...and be encouraged to know that you don't have to deal with problems on your own. Casting all your care upon him; for he careth for you. I Peter 5: 7. May the grace of God surround you in the abundance of peace, joy and happiness.

INTRODUCTION:

Dear Reader:

To understand yourself is a very difficult task, it often takes a lifetime to realize and know with a sense of assurance and security just who you really are. Our course in this present world has many uncertainties and because of our bad judgment, we often select the paths that lead to detours of the unexpected... down the road we run head on into trouble. Without any explanation of how we have arrived at this point, not really understanding what has happen we are faced to deal with consequences and dangerous situations that ultimately has caused us to loose valuable and productive time in our lives.

We make many mistakes, we stumble and fall... not recognizing that we fall too much and stay down too long. Due to our own faults and inabilities and not being able to determine actually what we should be accomplishing at this particular time in our lives, we reach a dry and empty place. We feel the isolation and despair and then suddenly...we discover that we are lost, layered with emotions and without God. Our own consciousness makes us feel guilty. You ask yourself questions and it's apparent that you don't have the answers...as you attempt to make yet another adjustment, you have lost sight of a brighter tomorrow. A day filled with love, joy and hope...seems to be gone.

From deep within you hear questions pounding at your mind, it's like a puzzle and you're faced with a dilemma because you have no true concrete answers to support the reasons why and how you have arrived at this particular destination. The missing pieces of your puzzle force you and anyone to deal with the hidden pain and the reality that you don't know yourself very well after all. For some, you have not established a relationship with God!!! He is the One that fills the longing of your soul.

If you have accepted Jesus Christ and His anointing into your life you will have wisdom and knowledge. God's Word will lead and guide your course in this life and His Holy and Divine Power will give you new abilities and power and might to become "sons and daughters" in Christ Jesus. Once the dynamic power and awesome spirit of God abides and dwells on the inside of you; the scripture so states...that you are a new creature in Christ. (II Corinthians 5:17 says: Therefore if any man be in Christ, he is a new creature: old things are passed away; behold, all things are become new.)

Without God you can do nothing!!! Think about that statement...without God you can do nothing and never will be complete. But with God all things are possible and through God you can do all things. Through His power and ability, you can do all... things!!!

Greater is He that is in you than he that is in the world. (I John 4:4 - Ye are of God, little children, and have overcome them: because greater is he that is in you, than he that is in the world.) God has a purpose and plan for your life...should you chose to accept, there is life and life more abundantly.

Should you deny that God is calling you with a spiritual call and awakening your soul to choose life, then death without hope is waiting for you. For the wages of sin is death, but the gift of God is eternal life through Jesus Christ. (Romans 6:23)

God is a merciful God filled with grace and truth. When you respond with a repented heart asking for the forgiveness of your sins, God is faithful to forgive you...at that very moment of all your sin. You don't have to wait or tarry or try to work towards being accepted or feeling worthy enough...believe God and ask Him to save you, accept Him as your Lord and Savior and He will never remember your sin again... He decides to forget, only to remember the great love that He has for you.

The answer that is on the inside...is God!!! He wants to direct you, to keep you and take you through the obstacles of life...God never leaves you alone. He won't turn His back on you when you need Him most. He is a very present help in our afflictions. (Psalm 46:1 - God is our refuge and strength, a very present help in trouble.) God did it all in the name of "Love"...For God so loved the world, that he gave his only begotten Son, that whosoever believeth in him should not perish, but have everlasting life. (St John 3:16)

Nobody knows what tomorrow holds...the future belongs to God. He is the same, yesterday, today and forever!!! Time is of the Lord.

Jesus allows us to know what His purpose for our lives should be. There is no doubt or confusing puzzle to figure out; He will reveal to us everything we need to know as we continue to seek Him in prayer daily, and stay in His Word. Be consecrated and dedicated to pursue God with your whole heart. As you seek to know the will of God for yourself, you will then understand by and by...one must first seek the kingdom of God. In the book of Matthew 6:33 it says, "But seek ye first the kingdom of God, and his righteousness; and all these things shall be added unto you." The answer to all of your problems can be solved and you will soon know that...The answer that is on the inside!!!

I have been tested and tried...I have walked out and lived to experience that "The Answer Is On The Inside." What God is allowing me to share with you in this book is absolute truth and if you will believe, His Word will not return back unto Him void...but it will accomplish an even greater work in you.

May God richly bless you with His Power...and give you the desires of your heart and bring your dreams into reality, the best is yet to come and your latter end shall be far better than your beginning. With Jesus on the inside you are victorious in every area of your life!!!

CHAPTER I
LIVING…TO LIVE AGAIN!!!

" I always believed… I could make it if I tried hard enough.
To give in any situation all of myself, the very best of me.
Having done what you could and no less… it does matter
a great deal…only you can't always see your own situation
clearly… and so you may be living, not understanding your
life!!!

This true story is based on my ordeals and former life style. I will divulge the experiences and openly convey my emotional state of being during that time. I will portray the difficulties that existed from the choices I made, later having to live and face so many issues, without God as the Head of my life. As I lived during that period of my life, I don't know how I made it. It truly was by the grace of God. My life and the way I lived was the actual process of bringing me into the knowledge of Jesus Christ and His Anointing!!! The Lord caused me to know Him in a personal way. I had to try Him for myself. As the scripture says, "Oh taste and see that the Lord is good; blessed is the man that trusteth in him. Psalm 34:8.

When a person has been raised and taught about the Gospel of Jesus, there is a deep understanding within that individual that is constant and will remain through the storms of life. As a young person, to be shaped and molded in the ways of God is extremely important. From the beginning of life, man was made in the image and likeness of God. You have a connected force that will lead and guide you into all truth. God is truth!!!

The scripture is so profound in Proverbs 22:6, which states: Train up a child in the way he should go: and when he is old he will not depart front it. Belief in God is rooted within the person and because of an early embrace to accept and believe in God this person will have the ultimate experience and walk with God. This individual perhaps will make mistakes in their lives, but they will always remember the principles of the doctrine, they will always know where to return, after they had tried everything else. But to God be the glory, for His mercy and forgiveness.

This is a foundational verse that supports an established character, with spiritual beliefs and values. Without guidance, rules and structure, and of course The Word of God as the source of authority; many people grow up lost, no righteousness or hope beyond their capabilities. They are void of an understanding of having received the revelation of who Jesus is. Without positive mentoring and Christian role models to demonstrate and live effective and holy lives we will lose many of our young people to the world. With all that we face today, this modern society needs to know how to live and how to practically seek God in your life.

Your life may not be happy or you still might be searching for love. You are looking for happiness, but in all the wrong places and from all the wrong people.

Without joy there is no genuine peace. Your mind is confused because there are too many questions left unanswered. It even shows on your face, your continence is so revealing. How do you honestly respond to those that feel they are closest to you and can help...You have made bad choices, the wrong choices and any decision in your life without Jesus to consult and to find out what is His will concerning the issue, will cause you trouble and pain. Some may say, "Well I'm a good person." But being good is not God's best and your moral opinion of yourself has nothing to do with accepting Jesus as your personal savior.

Without God you can do nothing...but with God all things are possible!!! I speak from my heart when I admit, that growing up I made so many mistakes. I had the "I don't care" attitude when there were problems I had to deal with. I know now that it was from a lack of spiritual wisdom and understanding and I needed to make the right adjustments and be ready to move on in a correct way!!! But I didn't have it all together, on the inside my spirit was empty and my soul was full of offense. I was very sad and yet I was able to cover my problems from everyone and especially those who were closest to me, by wearing a smile. I just always seem to have made the wrong decisions. I never could locate the pain I felt or feel the love I felt I deserved. It was really difficult to identify what the real problem was. It's called denial and I suffered from it for a long time...because I refused to realize, that I had a serious problem and I needed help and that I wasn't able to do it alone. You must be strong to admit that you indeed have a problem and willing to ask and seek help so that you can get back to the right path that leads to life. There is an abundant life, which is freely given by God...but we have to make the choice to accept God in our lives. We can choose life or death, good or evil... it's up to you!!! I decided to give Jesus a try!!! It took me a while to learn that Jesus wanted me on His side. I always wanted a better life. Now that I am saved and have given my life to the Lord, I do have an abundant life, I have eternal life now...I don't have to wait until I get to heaven...the kingdom of God is here now and wherever He is that is where I want to be.

By the age of 17, I was developed in my decision process. I had a focused determination and an inner ability to stand up for what I personally believed. I expressed my opinions seriously and people were aware that I meant what I said. In my character I had a quality to never give up for what I believed in and if anyone felt to convey to me that I couldn't accomplish my own desires, well...it was fuel to the soul and it gave me more strength to do the attainable. In the next few paragraphs I'll share with you my mind set as a very young girl. I wanted to set standards for myself and on purpose I set limits for myself. I decided that there were certain things that I would never do...I created some limits and boundaries for myself which was a good thing in keeping me strong. But somewhere along the way, I could sensed that my actions weren't all motivated by me alone. There was always a good part of me that seem to be unshaken or unmovable, even though I made a few bad choices along the way.

I never wanted to be like the majority, I simply had to be me. I could think rationally and make decisions for myself, without being led or influenced by others. It made me be more accountable and responsible for my actions because if I failed...I would be the one to blame.

Growing up I remember how pretty I thought my mother was to me. She had beautiful skin and simply an attractive lady. She had a small mole on her face and at that time it was a trend for women to have a "beauty mole" by their nose or on the chin area. She would highlight her beauty mole with a dark eyebrow pencil to really make it stand out ever so naturally. I thought I looked very much like my mother...but I never wanted to be like her...I never tried to emulate her ways or speak in her tone of voice. I was true to myself and believed that this was a great strength that I had produced. But it was really God working on me, I just wasn't aware as to how much He had to do with me!!!

I have much love and respect for my mother she raised me well and gave her best. Your foundation in life means everything, we didn't have an abundance of material things but we grew up with discipline, order and a clean home. She cooked dinner everyday, she was from the south and her style of cooking was always from "scratch," as we call it. She learned a lot from her grandmother, known as "Momma Cora," These were strong women and in the south, in those days you learned how to do what was needed to provide for your family.

I did not have a relationship with my natural father. I did not know him. I never saw him or do I have any memory of a relationship. That part of me, unfortunately I didn't have an opportunity to share and experience the love between a daughter and a father. But that's life...and so you handle and accept life for what it is and continue to move on in life. At the time of my father's death, however I was acknowledged, and someone remembered at this point... that he had a child. He resided in California and we received a telephone call late one night expressing the bad news and surprisingly they were calling to invite me to attend the funeral services. My mother spoke and relayed the message, I decided for myself...not to attend. I never knew him...nor shared my life with him and now death had separated us forever...I said my own goodbye in the privacy of my bedroom. I cried that night for a father I never knew, saw or touched...I cried knowing now that he was gone I would never get the chance to experience a father's love.

My mother had years prior to this, re-married and my stepfather was the only father I knew. I remembered him taking me places and holding my hand, buying me ice cream, potato chips or anything I asked for...school shopping was like Christmas, he purchased everything I wanted and more. He took good care of me and protected me from the boys he thought weren't up to no good. He later co-signed for my very first car! What a great day that was...he made me very happy and I knew He didn't have to do it, but I realized that he loved me just like I really was his own child. Trust me, a child knows when they are loved and wanted or hated and despised. So, I'm thankful for my father, Barry Olson Randall and all he did for me. He gave of himself and his time. To me that was important and he left an impression worthy to be respected.

CHAPTER 2
LIVING THE "RIGHT WAY!"

Life brings swift transitions, often situations beyond our control. How we respond can affect our future, our hopes and dreams.

The way a man thinks...is a powerful force that allows an individual to stand, regardless of the circumstances around them. Or if he has no substance, or faith he surely will fall. Proverbs 23:7 states: For as he thinketh in his heart, so is he. With the right attitude and a focused mindset, nothing can impede your progress. When your way of thinking begins to align with the will of a sovereign God, we can step into new heights of understanding and obtain deeper depths of truth that will lead to an abundant way of living, a right way of living that is promised by God!!!

There is much to say about my past of which I must often refer back to in reference to this story. I attempted to do well in my life, but the unexplainable occurred and I made many unwise choices. It is believed that as you age, you will mature and be more responsible. As you travel through life, the day arrives when you are faced to deal with the consequences of your actions and you hope that you are mature enough to get your life in order. But, most of the time we are not responsible, mature adults. I wasn't prepared for the trouble I caused. Once I reached the crossroads of my life, I was driven to the point of handling the mistakes and trying to correct myself to become a productive and respectable person. But I seem to have created more problems. I always wanted to do my best and resolved within myself, that I could solve my own problems. That was far from true. I needed a lot of help and it took me years to discover that with God on the inside I would be able to both handle and solve any situation in my life.

I never blamed anyone for my faults and realized within myself once and for all; that I would never make the same mistakes twice. I would grow up and graduate from problems and learn from my difficulties. Well, I finally did grow up...and I discovered that you never graduate from the trials of life. You learn how to live and make the right choices that will lead to joy and happiness. This is my story...I go back in time to reveal how I moved forward in life.

In 1972, I was a senior at Northwestern High School, in the City of Flint, Michigan. I had prepared myself for college, but mentally I really didn't know what I wanted to do with my life. I wanted to pursue something of worth and greatness, but I didn't have an ideal of what I was suppose to achieve. No real purpose. When a student graduates it seems like they are expected to know exactly what they want to do with their life. Some do and many don't...I happened to be one, that didn't know what I was to become. If the truth be told, a person is only truly prepared when

10

they have sought the wisdom and mind of God for their lives!!! In his divine purpose He has a plan especially for you. But most of us bypass God and go with our own feelings, family beliefs and the advise of others.

In school, I received help from the guidance counselors. They arranged for me to take college prep courses. At the time, I had many interest and enough potential to be what ever I wanted to be...but it was all time consuming and was just too hard to figure out. I just wanted to go to college. I never thought to get advice or direction from God. I didn't know enough to seek God for wisdom and understanding as to what I should have done with my life at that point. I didn't know what to do. I wasn't focused on any particular path of study. I had so many questions... and no answers. I continued on as if everything would magically work itself out and this was my first serious mistake!!!

I did everything required to attend the college of my choice. I passed all my entrance exams and SAT test and every other test...the only thing that I didn't pass, was the need for financial aide support. How was I going to obtain enough money to go to college? This was bigger than me, or the funds that I didn't have in the bank!!! From some place inside of me, I found myself crying out to the Lord. This was something that was important to me and I needed help. I had no place to turn but to the Lord.

But it was just a matter of time, and one fine day in the mail...my answer came. I had been accepted at Eastern Michigan University in Ypsilanti, Michigan with a full scholarship, including room and board and meals and books at no extra cost to me!!! It was amazing...I was filled with tears of joy. This moment had changed my life...I just held the letter in my arms and thanked God for all he had done. I was so excited. This had been a dream come true!!!

Sorry to report, that excitement didn't last too long, in between paragraphs my life did change... when my senior graduation day arrived, I was already two months pregnant. I graduated in my cap and gown and very much with child. Everything I had worked so hard for, now suddenly appeared to be gone and not possible for me to obtain. To describe the pain and disappointment was a feeling that I had to bear alone. When you know that you're directly responsible for the dilemma you find yourself in...it hurts real bad. I had to face the fact that it was partly my fault...but it was my own behavior that put me in this situation and now I would pay for my discretion and disobedience to my parents. College was out of the picture. Now, I had to "think" about giving birth and raising a child on my own. I had to do what needed to be done. This was my second mistake. It was a mistake only because of the timing. I was only 17 and emotionally not ready for a child. I was very hurt and because of my actions the opportunity to attend Eastern University was gone just as quickly as this wonderful gift had been given to me. It was gone.

Now, I had a whole new set of problems and questions that not only affected me, but also my child. I played it over and over in my mind and I thought about what I had done and came to terms with the consequences of my sin. I admitted the wrong I had done and was so sorry for being out of order, and disobedient to my parents and most of all disobedient to God. I acknowledged God and asked for His forgiven. I made a sincere approach to God because I knew that this time I had really went to far. I was ashamed of myself, and the pain that I had caused even to myself. I didn't know very much about this mysterious God. But I sensed I had did him wrong too. In the past I had attended Sunday school and had read Bible stories about the miracles and mighty works that Jesus had performed. But I needed more than a spiritual rendition, to satisfy my soul. I was in trouble and I needed to know if He was there...to heal my wounds and restore the right spirit within me.

I reviewed my church history, and my life and I came to the realization that I never had established a personal relationship with God!!! Jesus was not introduced to me as the Living God that knows all, (omniscient) and has all power, (omnipotent) and is everywhere at the same time, (omnipresent). I didn't know him as a loving Saviour, Lord or Friend. I stood before Him empty. I realized that I had no real connection with Him and I would be judged for sure.

I can speak from experience when I say that I had to put my trust in God during a difficult period in my life when I wasn't certain of my beliefs. Although I didn't know God the following scriptures became alive in me: Proverbs 3:5 and 6 says, Trust in the Lord with all thine heart; and lean not unto thine own understanding. In all thy ways acknowledge him, and he shall direct thy paths. I had to reach out to God. I didn't know much about the Word at the time, but Isaiah 55:6 it says to... seek ye the Lord while he may be found, call ye upon him while he is near. In my heart, I spiritually gave the Lord permission to take control and become the head of my life. I had too many burdens to bear.

I sought the Lord and He heard me and delivered me from all my fears. (Psalm 34:4). Even though I didn't have a great deal of information about God, I used what I had and that was the spirit that was on the inside of me, directing me to seek after his strength and his wisdom and He would provide. In my own way, I talked to God like a child talks to their earthly father. My words were uninhibited and I gave all my burdens and all my cares to God. My mind, my conscience and every secret thought needed to be cleansed. There's nothing to hard for the Lord and I wanted to be delivered from the guilt of my pregnancy.

The more I cried out for help, the more the Lord began to restore. He touched my life in a supernatural way and He delivered my mind and brought clarity of my thoughts. In Psalm 23:3 it says, "He restoreth my soul: he leadeth me in the paths of righteousness for his name's sake." The Lord did that for me. In a time of trouble...He heard me and delivered me from all my fears...I knew then, that God was watching over me. I woke up one day and had new determination, I felt encouraged and I had a better attitude about my situation. I believed I would be all right and that I would be able to take good care of my child. This was a break through. He allowed me to pass through my personal sufferings and to see that going to college would not be a far distant dream, but one day a soon reality. It was a temporary delay, but I wasn't denied. One day it would happen, I would attend college and provisions would be there to help me receive a degree.

At 17, it was not easy having a child out of wedlock, but I had God watching over me and He would supply all my needs. Is there anything to hard for the Lord? No!!! There is nothing impossible with God!!! I believed it and had faith in God. I was getting closer to God. I knew him as God…He gave me peace and assurance that life is a gift and nothing catches Him unaware or by surprise. My daughter, Monique belonged to God. I loved her, but God loved her best and with the Lord watching over us, we would be fine.

In 1976, I was accepted to attend Delta College in University Center, Michigan. I was awarded a 2- year scholarship. The promise of God came to pass…once again, for a second time I had the opportunity to begin a field of study of my choice!!! I had plans and I felt the desire to succeed was within my reach…the power was in my hands and in my heart, I knew I could do it…Being accepted at Delta was a leap of faith in the right direction. But I had to consider so much. I had a lot to decide. When you are faced with so many issues and questions that you don't quite know how to resolve, you need to know where you can run too for help. I came to an understanding that God knows what to do…through my past experiences I believed that God would work it out. I put my problems in God's hand. I felt like the Lord knew more about me than I did…and He was doing a great job!!! He knows what is on the inside of each of us!!!

In the Book of Job, chapter 38, God questions Job. Job had been chosen and elected to suffer for the glory of God. Our God is forever faithful and His word is tried, tested and true. What He has promised that is exactly what He will do!! The Book of Job is a recorded example that God can take us through the best days as well as through the difficult seasons of uncertainties in our lives. We must keep the "faith of God," and resist the motivation of doing things our way. If we are steadfast in our commitments to God, recognizing that the Lord is well able to handle any situation, the battle is over. When we surrender to the Lord and let Him fight on our behalf, victory is certain and we win!!! Whatever the Bible says...you can say...because the word will never fail and it will never change. In Psalms 119:89 it says, "Forever, O Lord, thy word is settled in heaven. The Lord Jesus Christ can never fail and He has commenced a wonderful work inside of those that believe. You will always need Him. He is there to embrace us in his divine love that has no limits or conditions. It is by His mercy and grace that we have made it this far. In Acts 17:28 it affirms that, for in him we live, and move, and have our being...for we are also his offspring. Jesus loves us and we are very much a part of Him as He is a part of us.

CHAPTER 3
TO KNOW HIM

In any relationship you must spend time with that person to know them…

For me, I personally felt that I was being drawn closer and closer to the Lord. He heard my cry and He knows the end from the beginning…even before the foundations of the world…God knew me!!! I had a change in my attitude and behavior. It is so amazing to me now…because I recognize that the Lord has a plan designed especially for each of us. We all just come from different backgrounds in life. But He provides all our needs and sustained us with a protection that is secure "in spite of ourselves. "

You can't figure God out!!! He will not fit into our pattern of thinking. He has said, "For my thoughts are not your thoughts, neither are your ways my ways, saith the Lord." (Isaiah 55:8). He allows us to have a free will and spirit equipped with our own unique personality and characteristics. Jesus is the life giver… He is life eternal. And the Lord God formed man of the dust of the ground, and breathed into his nostrils the breath of life and man became a living soul. (Genesis 2:7) Once you accept Jesus in your life and have been filled with the Holy Ghost, according to Acts 2:38 or some prefer to say, the Holy Spirit...then we have been redeemed by the blood of the Lamb and accepted by the Beloved, that we are truly sons and daughters of God!!!

He knows each one of us by name. We have got to come to the place, where we know him and in the pardon of our sins. I soon learned to call Him Jesus. That is his saving name. It is the name I love to call him by. God told Moses... I AM THAT I AM...tell pharaoh that I AM sent you...whatever you may perceive God to be, He is much more than you may identify with or people recognize Him to be. He is more than a popular icon of historical times, He is more than the sacrifice that died on that old rugged tree...the point is...who do you say that He is and what does he mean to you? Our words alone can't describe Him. We are unable to conclude all of who and what He is! His awesomeness goes beyond comprehension and there is no limit to what He can do, and how He can do it...

What do you call Him? Moses needed to know... whom should I say sent me? By what authority gives me the right to stand before great men? God spoke... I AM THAT I AM!!! Later, pharaoh would know by God's terrible acts and there would be no need for questions. Pharaoh would know that the, I AM OF HEAVEN AND EARTH was God! Many times in our lives we don't recognize who God is...but when He shows up in the middle of our troubled lives and saves us with a tender hand of love and mercy we know that we have been rescued by His grace and unmerited favor. We speak out of the abundance of our hearts and proclaim with our mouth who He is!!! Romans 10:10 says: For with the heart man believeth unto righteousness; and with the mouth confession is made unto salvation. This is all I had and I believed just as the scripture repeats in Romans 10:11, whosoever believeth on him shall not be ashamed.

God is whatever He wants to be. What is so fascinating is that, He can be whatever you need Him to be. He is the truth, the light, and the way. He is the door by which all must go through. He is ever precious. He is Love!!! But without faith it is impossible to please him: for he that cometh to God must believe that he is, and that he is a rewarder of them that diligently seek him. (Hebrews 11:6) He is a forgiver, a supplier, a keeper and sustainer too! He is sweeter than the honey in the honey cone and arrayed in beauty that's all together lovely. He is nearer and closer than when you first believed. He is alpha and omega, the beginning and the end. He is the King of Kings and Lord of Lords. The great I AM…JESUS is his name. He is my Father!!! He is the solid rock that will never lose its power. He is water in a thirsty land and bread for the hungry. He will give you water that you will never thirst again and food which is manna from on high. He is a guide that can lead you all the way…He is joy in sadness and comforter in your troubles. He said He would stick closer than a brother and would never leave or forsake you. He is the healing balm, your shield and buckler. He is our great sufficiency. He is the ONE that saves…

Don't buy into the hype that you can live anyway you choose and do whatever you want to do. Don't be fooled…God always knows!!! He has a standard of living called holiness. Seek the Lord and His righteousness and everything you need will be added. In the Book of Matthew 6:31 and 32 it states: Therefore take no thought, saying, "What shall we eat? Or, What shall we drink? Or, Wherewithal shall we be clothed?" For after all these things do the Gentiles seek: for your heavenly Father knoweth that ye have need of all these things. But seek ye first the kingdom of God, and his righteousness; and all these things shall be added unto you. Never pattern your life after others, but mark the perfect man, for after that man...is peace. (Psalm 37:37) Seek God for your life. Ask the Lord, What would He have you to do. In prayer, request for direction, wisdom and knowledge. Seek the Lord for guidance and the ability to hear the voice of God. Read his word and find yourself in the scriptures. All the answers to your complicated situations can be solved, but you must begin to put God first and acknowledge him in all your ways... and He will direct your life. I had to reach one of the lowest points in my life to discover the love of Jesus. The power of God is constantly abiding in our midst and Jesus wants to dwell on the inside of every person. He holds your future and destiny in his will, with the Lord Jesus you can face tomorrow with confidence and faith. He is the problem solver and He instructs us to cast all our cares upon Him for He cares for us. (I Peter 5:7). Remember the battle has already been won!!! You have the victory...only believe and have faith. Let the power of God work in you.

CHAPTER 4
GOD SPEAKS

…He will reveal himself to you.

God speaks in Job 38. Let's consider verse 36, Who hath put wisdom in the inward parts? Or who hath given understanding to the heart? The Hebrew word for wisdom is chakham, meaning to be wise, intelligent, to be prudent, become wise, make wise; to teach, to be cunning; clever or to show oneself wise. Hebrew wisdom was very different from other ancient world views. Israel believed that there was a personal God who was and is Holy and just and that He expects us to live our lives according to His principles. They emphasized the human will of the heart, not the intellect that a person had acquired in the head. Therefore the Hebrew wisdom was very practical and was based on what God revealed about right and wrong. This all applied to daily life. The true wisdom is always used in a positive sense. True wisdom leads to reverence for the Lord!! This is why this wisdom is on the inside, within the soul of the person, so that when realization and spiritual revelation comes…the person that has been searching and seeking justly in conquest of the realities of divine living will find true purpose and meaning in their lives. It is within this journey that a person begins to discover Jesus with inquisitive motivations. When bits and pieces of revealed information about God is obtained, inside of us the light of our understanding is then turned towards God and by and by you began to understand. As you move into God's righteousness, you then turn to God with repentance of heart because you want to forsake your ways. When you arrive at this new point in your life…it's all about Jesus, less of you and more and more of Him.

You will yield your life to God with a surrendered heart and mind. Your praise and worship to God is real and your life has purpose and meaning. You are dedicated to service and you honor the Lord for the unique work that God has done to establish you in the faith. Then life demands answers, in which time will explain. But there is an inward truth and like Job you will know the answers for yourself, because the transformation of what God has done in your life will always cause you to respond in belief to God because you know for yourself that He is real.

Jobs prosperity was restored in Job 42:10 "And the Lord turned the captivity of Job, when he prayed for his friends: also the Lord gave Job twice as much as he had before. When your friends mistreat you and count you out…keep doing what the Lord has put in you to do. Love those that despitefully hurt you. Strive to do right and please God, keep His commandments and you will be an instrument that God can use; the day will come when you will have to pray for those that have done evil against you. The Lord knows how to restore and bless and give you double for your trouble. Job 42:12 reads: So the Lord blessed the latter end of Job more than his beginning: for he had fourteen thousand sheep, and six thousand camels, and a thousand yoke of oxen, and a thousand she asses. God is faithful and His promises are true. Just you wait on God and He will surely bring it to past. Trust in the Lord and He will work it out in his season. He is never late and always on time!!! If you will trust and obey God his blessings will overtake you and your expected end will be greater than your beginning. But there needs to be a relationship with God. You must accept him into your heart and He will always be there for you.

In many of my own life experiences I soon realized that the source to all the problems in which I faced, the answers always came from inside of me. The closer I got to God…the clearer truth became. It was real truth, valid and most sacred truth; an awareness that only the Creator can give. My understanding was open and my mind was free of confusion to make decisions that were positive, good and wholesome for me. The closer to God I got the more God began to reveal. My heart was touch and moved to respond with acceptance and my inner being wanted more of this great God. I needed so much more and my soul commenced to hunger and thirst after God's righteousness. I looked at myself without the aide of a mirror and could see how empty I was. My life was not dedicated to God and my soul, the real me; was not covered in the eternal glory of the Almighty. I needed the Love of God to be manifested in my life!!!

I began to ask myself definite questions, because I wanted answers. I had often heard people say that they are the "captain" of their lives. They say that, they control their destiny and can make things happen, when they want them to happen. But without the knowledge of God in your life; how can a person talk about the things of God, the future; tomorrow or destiny? Only God, The Lord, Jesus Christ holds tomorrow's destiny, dreams and your life in his control. We say so many things that sound good, but they have no merit. We are not the captains of our lives, nor are we the head of our lives. We are not in control of our lives and we barely can handle the day- to- day affairs of business. Our lives do not measure up to the standards of God. Our family structure is a wreck, dysfunctional and totally out of order and not the will of God for many families today. The sole providers should be the parents, but are not and our children are suffering as a result. Our morals are now…no morals and it seems as if the fear of God has been removed from human consciousness. We say we love one another and hurt the ones most dear to us…we kill and soon forget!!! How can we be captains of our lives when we don't even know from whence we came or where we are headed? We are lost and have no spiritual awareness of what's going on…today, digital satellite can give our location, handle human mistakes and even predict the weather, but do you know if you are traveling on the path in life? On the inside where it counts most, can you feel when something is wrong? Without God we have no earthly direction of the way in which we should go. Without God how can a person know? We give him hardly any of our time, and take no time to plan. We have no plans with purpose and no vision to see beyond ourselves. But there is a way out. Jesus is the answer and the way. If we would take the time to seek God and pray...He tells us to humble ourselves and pray, and then shall we hear from Heaven. Open the Bible and ask God for understanding of his word. If any man seeks wisdom let him ask God.

So very often we believe that we are so sure of ourselves and think we know how to solve the issues that complicate our existence. But honestly, we really don't know what is best and create more problems from the decisions that we continue to make. But we can hope in God because He will never fail!!! We must get in the presence of God and seek to know what His divine will is for our lives and the direction that He wants us to take. We are precious in the sight of the Lord, born with talents and natural god-given abilities. He has empowered us to prosper so that His covenant will be established in the earth. (Deuteronomy 8:18) He ordains the callings and gifts. It is he that anoints and appoints, he brings down one...and promotes another. All power is given unto Him. He is a righteous God of all the earth and He will do right!!! Once we surrender to Jesus and allow Him to have preeminence in our life and simply say, YES in obedience to His every command, we begin a spiritual and Christian race; which requires each one of us to know our purpose and reason for being on this earth. Our faith is established in the foundation of Jesus Christ and we are true disciples in the Word of God. The Lord will map out our course and direction and assign us to stay in our own lane, specifically a path that the Lord has chosen and set before us to run...

and to run this race with patience. As He speaks, we begin to live with hope that goes beyond this present world, we press for the mark of the high calling of Christ Jesus!!! Striving to enter into God's rest, and to endure until the end.

Jesus will give you wisdom, if you ask. James 1:5 instructions, If any of you lack wisdom, let him ask of God, that giveth to all men liberally, and upbraideth not; and it shall be given him. The Lord wants you to get wisdom and understand and forget it not; neither decline from the words of his mouth. Proverbs 4:5. The Lord will supply all our needs and sustain us with his power to cause us to be victorious in every area of our lives. But we must have a prayer life in which we allow the Almighty God to speak to us and give us the directions we need. He knows the way in which we should take and all our faith and trust should be in the Lord Jesus Christ and the power of his anointing. So, we continue to run this race until the end.

At some point in our lives, because time and chance happens to us all, we may fall and commit sin...against God!!! God hates sin and will not have any fellowship with sin. We must learn to honor the Lord with our very lives and live just like the Bible teaches. There is no peace with God when we fail to obey his commandments, statues and ordnances. The condition of our heart should be filled with repentance as you approach the Lord with forgiveness. All unrighteousness is sin (I John 5:17). Only the Lord can carry our sorrows and lift our burdens and judge us according to his word. Don't live beneath the standard of holiness. Never live and continue in sin, but come boldly to the throne of grace, that we may obtain mercy and find grace in a time of need. (Hebrews 4:16) You will never know what the end will be if you don't finish the race. Be encouraged to continue and never look back, once you've been forgiven. Yes, there have been painful situations that have occurred in the lives of many believers, but joy always comes in the morning. I John 1:9 declares that if we confess our sins, he is faithful and just to forgive us our sins, and to cleanse us from all unrighteousness. A quitter never wins and a winner never quits!!! You and only you can determine how long it takes to get to "your morning!" The race is not given to the swift, but to he that endures until the end. We sometimes view ourselves by the accomplishments of others and attempt to duplicate their successes. But you never know the true story behind what many people have gone through in order to reach that place in life where they feel that they are successful. You don't know the obstacles they had to deal with, the hills they had to climb to reach their destiny, only to face failure and disappointments. How many times did they pursue the dream, only to discover that the cost was too great and they had to give up; or for some, they decided never to surrender!!! Who was there to encourage them and give support? You don't know the race that they had to run…in pursuit of victory, you don't even know if they obtained their goals honestly or had the favor of God!!! So, never judge yourself by others; but seek to know the will of God for your life.

It is a necessary process that a "child of God" must go through. Each person must seek God for himself and let your prayers make a fervent connection with the intimacy of the Lord. A personal relationship is one that we never want to loose and our dialog with God is continual. We must speak and confess and declare for yourself. You can never determine the price that anyone pays to make it to the place of success. You don't realize what struggles they overcame to achieve their goals. But, you can talk with God for yourself and quietly listen as He talks to you...your prayer time should not only contain the desires of your heart and the petitions to God, but also the hidden secrets of your heart; expressed by speaking in the spiritual language of the Holy Ghost. The established Word of God should be directed back to the one that promised...now unto him that is able to do exceeding abundantly above all that we ask or think, according to the power that worketh in us. (Ephesians 3:20) It's important to say what the Word of God says!!! The Lord honors His Word...not your tears, fears or the thunderous presentation of your speech to get his attention...But God honors His Word and will fulfill that which He has promised. As you continue to seek God you must have faith...the scripture in Hebrews 11:6&7 says, "But without faith it is impossible to please him: for he that cometh to God must believe that he is, and that he is a rewarder of them that diligently seek him." You must believe that God is...without question. His Word is forever settled in Heaven. Psalm 119:89. There is nothing too hard for him. He can do the impossible and all things are possible to him that believes. Have faith to claim the promises of God.

CHAPTER 5
THE CROSSROADS TO NEW LIFE

You may have walked many paths in this journey of life.
Some roads will lead to success while others may cause you
to never reach your goals.

With Christ as the Head of your life, your road trip has already been ordained before the foundation of the world. It is your mission, should you choose to accept, to arrive at your intended destination safely!!!

Many times God is orchestrating situations and allowing circumstances in our lives to put us on the path of life that He has purposed for us. I am reminded of a very important time in my life that seem to have caused me great confusion, but in reality it was a crossroad; which was but a brief moment in time that changed my life and put me on the right path...to life.

It was one night at college, during a casual party in which most of us were just hanging out, listening to music and talking and having fun with friends. There were some people there that I was not acquainted with and I was introduced and soon engaged in the topic of discussion. Everything was interesting...and perhaps I was a bit excited to be participating in such a collegiate format. I'm a proud freshman!!! The music produced a nice mood, the atmosphere was great... and as I glanced around the room my eye caught sight of a beautiful picture, it was different from all others that I had seen like it. I had to get a closer look. As I stood there focused on the picture, I thought to myself what a beautiful picture of Jesus...others noticed me just standing in front of the portrait, they wanted to know what was so special about it. I expressed how beautiful I thought this picture of Jesus was!!! And suddenly the whole atmosphere and groove in the room changed, the music stopped like the scratching of a LP; and everyone was starring at me...as if I had said something that was damaging and unforgivable!!! Quickly people took sides and there was a division in the room. Clearly a different point of belief from everyone, of whom they thought the picture was depicting; nobody really had a name and yet, we could not agree on who the person in the picture was. A debate arose that separated us and some were to angry to remain. All because the truth hurts and nobody in the room had enough truth to defend themselves and what they believed. Who actually was in the picture? God, Jesus or The Lord Almighty or was it the Black Madonna?

The picture I saw was beautiful and my heart would not deceive me, I knew it was Jesus in that picture. But that night I was not filled with enough true of my own to know for sure without any doubt who Jesus really was and be able to intelligently explain, why to others. I questioned myself and tried to identify the times I had learned about God in church and heard preachers call on the name of Jesus and remembered stories of the older mothers giving thanks to the Lord. But there was no connection, no relationship in which I could clearly identify with. I remembered my recent past experiences, but I didn't have the knowledge of a biblical education. I'm in college now...I've got to give some proof and reason for my conclusions, I needed to show some scriptures, but at this point, I had never really studied the Bible. I knew Jesus and I must have met God someplace and how did He become Lord? I wasn't sure and for the first time I was moved out of my comfort zone to inquire more about who Jesus was. I didn't have scriptures for my friends that night. I admit, I was not deep into the Word, it would be hard to defend my feelings with this group. They needed more than conversation. When I looked at the picture, it was as if the picture I saw was looking at me and asking me the questions, "... are you saved...why won't you come unto me...are you on the right road...Who do men say that I am, Who do you say...I AM!!!"

When I left the party, my whole spiritual attitude was down. I was empty on the inside. I wasn't for sure who I was after that get together!!! If I didn't know who God really was how could I begin to understand who I was? I was going to have to make some drastic changes to get to the bottom of the questions that were facing me again. I just felt so troubled by not knowing the truth about Jesus. How would I find the "right" answers, there are so many religions today, how could I satisfy this feeling I now had on the inside. I was sick...some would say sin sick. What type of medicine could take this pain away? I continued to see that picture of Jesus in my head for the longest time. There seem to be no escaping it and all I could do was to ask Jesus to help me understand Him better. That is what was inside of me, I don't know where it came from...but the name of Jesus was alive in me and I held on to what was true within my own spirit. He would have to reveal Himself!!!

The crossroads of life will meet you wherever you happen to need the change. If you are sensitive to the inner voice within you, there will be no mistake when God calls you into a new twist or turn. The Lord will bring experiences in our lives for His purpose and our salvation. I was headed for repentance, and I didn't have a clue, that was what I needed all the time. I soon discovered that the repentance towards God was a great thing...a portion of scripture in Romans 2:4, states...not knowing that the goodness of God leadeth thee to repentance. Many people don't know the importance in the power of true repentance. It starts way before you ever reach church!!! God begins to draw you closers to Him, as you get closer to God your heart changes and you respond differently about the issues of life. Your mind thinks more on a spiritual level and you are more responsive to the calling of God!!! You can receive some revelation, simply because you hunger and thirst after righteousness and your soul is eager to be touched by God. The Bible declares in Matthew 4:4 and this is Jesus speaking, "It is written, that man shall not live by bread alone, but by every word that proceedeth out of the mouth of God." Now, what is important is that you have a desire to align yourself with the word of God and to come boldly to the throne of grace. In Hebrews 4:16

the scripture reads as follows, Let us therefore come boldly unto the throne of grace, that we may obtain mercy, and find grace to help in time of need. Finally, you have come to yourself and realize that you do need the Lord Jesus Christ and his anointing power. His mercy and grace, his protection and most of all...you need his love!!! Repentance will cause your desires to change and habits to disappear. You can be delivered and free from all sin.

Suddenly you start to move towards God, you have left yourself behind!!! It is not your will...but God's will be done in you. Then in your search to get to God, the urgency of your mission compels you to get to him soon. You must thank Him for sparing your life and keeping you all these years from all harm and hidden dangers. You must surrender your all and bow before His presence in forgiveness. Repentance will let an individual see their past, all you have done and what you have not accomplished, but should have. When your past is directly before you it can be deplorable as you review all the ugly sins and transgression, there seems to be a fresh recording of all the wrong and evil acts that you committed and participated in. Like a movie your life is on the big silver screen, it's a true story and you know it actually happened. You question...did this truly happen...you had the leading role of course you know you were the star of the show!!! You look around to blame someone, anybody, for letting this information out; but guilt stands like a brick wall before you and you can't get around it no matter how you try. You are for once speechless, you apparently are choking for words... you want to speak and defend yourself, but this is not the time, it's a "silent" movie...no words allowed!!! In your mind you attempt to play the scene another way, but it's too late because you wrote the story yourself!!! Now you hear...it's a rap...it's over, it's finished!!! There you stand a lone, you begin to cry...and to cry uncontrollably, at this point you don't care who may be looking; you must reach God for his mercy, you don't care...you need his help. You can hardly wait to say you're sorry and to ask for a chance to do things differently, to be better than before...to ask for his forgiveness for the sins that you have done against his word and against your own body; which was given to you by God. Your body is not your own...it belongs to God and that is why you must give an account to the deeds done in "your body"...and tears of repentance fall...and down on your knees...you fall in submission calling on Jesus to save your soul from death, hell and destruction. He said that every knee would bow and every tongue confess, that Jesus Christ is Lord!!! You plead for mercy, for grace and healing of your body, soul and spirit. This is repentance and it works your soul, until you come to Jesus.

To everything there is a season and a time to every purpose under the heaven. Ecclesiastes 3:1. It takes a unique person to examine yourself and identify honestly the issues that face you. The objectives being that there are problems and circumstances that on our own we have not been able to solve. We have complicated our situations and caused major problems within our homes and between our families. While still expecting that things will suddenly change one day, and everything will be all worked out.

Far too long we have overlooked the power of God. We go everywhere looking for help and assistance. We search for a ready ear to listen and then advise us. We pay for therapy…twelve sessions if need be!!! We look in the yellow pages for the professionals and specialist. We tell our parents all our business, knowing that they can't be impartial to the situation. We speak in confidence to anyone that will listen. But we never stop to consider God…to seek after His council and His way of doing things. We don't even think to simply ask…God for His help!!! We can petition God for His instructions in righteousness. If we would seek God more we would avoid a lot of trouble. His deliverance and protection is ready and available. If any of you lack wisdom, let him ask God, that giveth to all men liberally, and upbraideth not; and it shall be given him. (James 1:5). But, for some unforeseen reason we never stop to get the wisdom of God…to ask the Lord in our private habitation to let His will be done in us. We must learn to admonish him for our purpose in life, because He knows what is best for each of us. We must begin to think of the advantages of being lead by God and to settle within our hearts that we trust Him. He is with us and we must have the faith to believe that He will carry us through. He created us…and He knows all about us. But yet we fail to recognize the greatest power on earth is available, and free of charge!!! Silver and gold is not the exchange. This kind of knowledge cannot be purchased with money. But love was the primary reason that caused God to come all the way from glory and prepare Himself a body in the person of the Lord Jesus Christ, to be our perfect example… and save us from sin. Money could never have made this purchase. Only the blood of Jesus could pay the price. He was in the world, but not of the world, He was without sin; and yet it pleased the Father that He should taste death in that He died on Calvary's Cross for all mankind...He died a death on the tree like no other ever recorded in history. Jesus died for you. He became a living sacrifice without spot or wrinkle, prepared and born to die. He was a perfect sacrifice that had to die...and yet he had no sin!!!

He was innocent, and He shed his blood for the remission of our sin. It was all for you...we are the heritage of the Lord, precious in His sight. He loves each one of us in particular because; we are His children. His heritage. We say that we love Him with our lips, but our hearts are far from Him. We show how much we love Him by our obedience and faith. Will we ever stop to hear what the spirit is saying... is there is a word from the Lord? Take the time to find out. It only takes one word to set you free!!!

CHAPTER 6
A PROMISE

God always remembers when we forget!!!

During the final months of my college days I had to reckon with the promise I had previously made to God and myself. It was embedded deep within the portals of my memory and my mind had the control to repeat what I had previously confessed and to constantly play it like a recording. I seem to be headed for one thing only and it was that this journey was about to steer me into the right pathway of life. I was at the crossroads and as I have often heard the saying... most people will one day arrive at the "decision" of the crossroads. Your life will automatically take you there. I was about to cross over into a way of living that would change my life forever.

Time was passing by quickly and now I was ready to change my lifestyle. I was in search of God...I felt that I needed Him and it was time to get acquainted with "The Master," of my soul. I had an unsettling feeling working inside of me and I knew it was time. It made me feel nervous with anticipation that something was about to happen. I wanted a personal relationship with "The Creator." I was ready to meet the One that was responsible for everything that exists...which included me!!! I had made this promise to God at the beginning of my college days and I vowed as much as I knew...that I would give my life to Christ. I promised Him that if, He would take me successfully through college and allow me to graduate, I would give my life to the Lord!!! It was a real heartfelt commitment because I realized that, the Lord was the reason I had survived all the troubles that I had experienced. He was with me all the time. I owed my life to The Lord and truly believed that all I could honestly give... was myself!!! It was an intense feeling that remained constant in my spirit and I knew that all Jesus really ever wanted was for me to accept Him. After realizing all that, I was glad I was still alive to see the day approaching and wonderful things began to happen as I gradually made my calling and election sure.

In 1978, I still had to complete a few more required courses. I attempted to count up the cost and realized it would be best to finish the remaining credits by commuting from home instead of living on campus. It was taking me so long to graduate, but I was determined not to quit. I would have all the credits to graduate in the spring of 1979. Then...as I had promised, I would give my life to the Lord. It doesn't matter how difficult life may be. I learned that it all depends on how determined you are and how you deal with the situation. I had many ups and downs to deal with in order to finish with a degree. I had to keep my purpose in my view, no matter how long it took. On April 29, 1979, I finally graduated from Delta College with a, Associate In Business Studies in Medial Assistant. I finished what I started.

My very first Sunday after graduation, I went to a holiness church I was invited by Evangelist Amanda Taylor, my daughter's great-grandmother. I had never been to a sanctified church and agreed to attend the service. God was up to something...I wore my black cap and grown from the college graduation and to my sweet surprise, people like graduates...but they love college graduates!!! I was treated with honor and was received with a warm embrace. Everyone wanted to shake my hand and offer congratulations. They were hugging and kissing me and the church photographer was happily snapping pictures and it was quite a touching moment. I felt the warmth of God's love through the people and I personally didn't know many of them and questioned my emotions, wondering how this could have such an affect on me.

I was in a position to hear from God. I was in the right place and I sensed the importance of being there. I wanted to have a relationship with God and had hoped my intentions were right. True repentance brings you into salvation and restores your soul with a clean heart. The spirit of God works on the inner man. God's wonders are performed inside the heart, mind and soul of a person. If any man will come after Jesus, he must first deny himself...Matthew 16:24. I was willing and ready to surrender everything. I had supernaturally been delivered from all the worldly habits even before I got to church...repentance was working and it put me in the place of a miracle and in the position to receive from God just what I needed most!!! I wanted to hear the voice of God... I was sure He would tell me what to do next...

As the service began to unfold, once again my mind replayed my promise that I had made to God, like a movie. This time it was clear as a rerun of the life that I had lived and how the Lord had allowed these ordeals to move me to a place where I would come to myself and acknowledge God as Lord. As The song service continued and I listened intently to all of it. The morning message was dynamic and I was in agreement with what was happening. I felt like one day, I would "join" church and give the Lord my life. I knew it was time to surrender, time to follow God and obey his word.

In the midst of my own world the spirit of God took control and the entire room was instantly filled with praise!!! You could feel the excitement and see the joy on the faces of the people. They were rejoicing, clapping their hands and some jumping up and down and others running around like they were on fire!!! Some sat quietly, but you could sense that it was tears of joy streaming down their cheeks. It was a joy that was contagious. I could see many people crying, but their face showed peace on their countenance. My heart was filled with love...I just had a sweeping feeling of love for everyone. This was bigger than me, and more about Jesus and what He wanted to accomplish in the lives of his people.

The church was like one big family and at that moment I felt like heaven was also rejoicing. I felt like I belonged and that I was a part of this huge church family that was celebrating because I had found my way home. I was touched and without any doubt I believed that I was in the right place at the right time.

I was home and the fact that everyone was so happy, dancing and shouting proved they were glad for me. It all wasn't about me...but I felt like it was a welcomed reception, pronouncing me to...come unto Jesus, ye that labor and are heavy laden, and I will give you rest. Take my yoke upon you and learn of me; for I am meek and lowly in heart; and ye shall find rest for your souls. My yoke is easy and my burden is light. (St. Matthew 11:28-30). A force was drawing me, pulling at my heart. God can do a quick work if we let him. We must be willing to receive it and believe it to allow the will of God to be done.

As the service ended, I was just happy...people were still taking my photograph and introducing themselves, they were so friendly and so kind. It must have been obvious to them that I had enjoyed myself and would be back for more!!! I didn't join church that Sunday, but the seed had been planted and even though I had not yet completed my part of the covenant, God still did not forsake me. It was a great day, a beautiful day. I had no ideal church people acted this way!!! It was a wonderful feeling that just overtakes your emotions...it was good to have been there. Whatever they had it was worth trying to get. I was transformed that day.

I had new desires and aspirations. I meditated about my life and becoming a Christian and what it would mean. My attitude was different because of what I had experienced at Bethlehem Temple of the Apostolic Faith, in the City of Flint, Michigan. God was doing a miraculous work on me and it started first at this assembly under the leadership of the late, Elder B.

T. Scott. I received light and wisdom from hearing the gospel preached. I realized that the Lord was working on the inside and once I would allow Jesus to come into my heart, I would never be the same.

Later, I was invited to attend a much smaller congregation on the east side of the city. Several weeks went by and then all of a sudden I decided to go. When I arrived I began to judge the church from the outside, it was a very small building and I guessed a small membership. It was nothing like the first church I had attended. But when I got inside...Oh... My God!!! I could feel that very same spirit present in the atmosphere as I had felt at the other church. The people were just happy and you could distinguish that they had something that I needed. They too, were friendly and very kind. I personally didn't know most of them and yet I was attracted spiritually. I could feel the warmth and genuine fellowship of the church members. I was treated with love and my pre-conceived opinion was worthless. You can't judge a book by its' cover...you have to open the book and read the contents and become familiar with the passages in order to evaluate and establish a valid conclusion. The church was small in number, but indeed served a big God. They had the love of Jesus in their hearts and that was enough for me.

I soon began to attend every service they had. I enjoyed every minute, every song and every sermon. I had no complaints and I was there both day and night, it didn't matter what day...I was there, I was in the house!!! A few months went by and something else started to occur. The messages of the preacher were working my soul, I was getting convicted and I needed to be baptized. I learned that I needed to receive the Holy Ghost. The church music was in me and I would be at home singing the lyrics and remembering the melody. I could remember everything. One fine day, they had a guest evangelist from Port Huron, Michigan. She was a preacher under the anointing of God and she ministered with power. It was so amazing to me...I was so captivated by the message she delivered. When the altar call was given, I started to cry, and I continued to cry. I couldn't stop myself. Repentance was at hand and this was it...it was time to give my life to the Lord and be saved!!!

But it was not that easy to do. Every evil force had to be at work instantly and I admit, I didn't know too much about the devil either...but clearly in a moment of time there was a war battling in my mind, in my spirit and in my body. Something was holding me down and it was stronger than my imagination, it was beyond my control. I tried to get up, but I couldn't move. I tried to talk and my mouth was sealed. I wanted someone, anybody to come and help me, but nobody responded. They didn't know the danger I felt and the fear that was on me. I wished, somebody had moved that day!!! I couldn't reach out and touch anyone, I tried to listen for a voice or whisper offering to come to my rescue; but nobody said a word!!! It was my move, but I was bound in my seat. It was as if there were chains that had weights attached and I was clamped in along with everyone around me. I was puzzled and afraid at the same time. I didn't know what was happening. I thought maybe I had waited to long or I must have done a great evil...what went wrong? Then, the altar call was over...I had the feeling like I had been in darkness and in a place of torment right in church. The lights appeared to be brighter and slowly I could move freely again. When I came to myself, I could see the people getting up and they were leaving, the service was over!!! I couldn't express what had just taken place. I was sure I wanted the power of God in my life, I was certain I was going to get what I had been in search of for some time. When I got outside, the weather was perfect...it should have been a glorious day for me and I started to cry again!!! I felt sorry for myself. I missed the best opportunity to save my own life...I missed it, what was I suppose to do now?

The evangelist that preached saw me crying. She approached me and put her arms around me. I believe the Lord Jesus allowed her to discern what I had experienced and she asked me, "why didn't you give up to Jesus?" Out of my own mouth, and I don't even know why, I told her, "I was not ready. I wanted to be saved, but I had some things I had to handle first." She said, "Honey, on your own you will never be ready to give your life to God and there is nothing so important that you must fix first." Nothing comes before God!!! She told me that I must come to Jesus just as I am. To surrender my will to Gods' will. She expressed to me that if we could make our situations right we would believe that we had no need for God. When she finished with me I had consolation. It was a relief to know that I wasn't obligated to solve all my problems. All that was required was that I believe, trust and obey my Father's voice and keep his word. He is the problem solver and had already given me the victory...I just didn't know it at the time.

That night I knew that Jesus truly loved me without any conditions. I didn't deserve the attention and the deliverance from the snares of evil, but the Lord saw fit to bless me in spite of myself. My soul had confirmation that I would get another chance to redeem myself, and the next time I would not let anything stop me.

CHAPTER 7
NEW LIFE

The Love of God is unconditional.

The cords to your heart come alive as you bid the Master a welcomed entry. An opened invitation that took years for you to respond to, and you finally make the decision to give God a try. In a moment of time you seem to be transformed. There is a part of us that longs to be filled with love and goodness and a joy that is heaven sent. Much of our lives we search for love. Agape love is the unconditional love of God. We want to be loved, but we fight against the reality that we need love in our life. Our heart and soul belongs to God!!! He can wipe away all fear and pain. There is not a person that can comfort our soul and add consolation like He can. He renews our spirit and restores the goodness that we once despised. If only we had known…how to come to Jesus sooner. I asked the Lord to forgive me of all my sin and grant me the power to overcome all the influences of evil. When I pray, I believe that he hears me and I trust that He will answer me. (I John 5:14 & 15)

I knew that somehow I would have to gather the courage to fight and be strong to gain what was rightfully mine. The enemy had put up several roadblocks to discourage me, but I began to have a different mindset and my determination allowed me to press towards the Lord and nothing or anyone would be able to stop me. This was my second chance. Yes…it was yet another opportunity to get to the Lord. It was a divine call, already planned and purposed by God. It was His doing and it was his hearts' desire that I would repent and be saved, giving my life to him as a vessel of honor. The devil himself could not stop me… but at the time I was not educated enough in the Word and didn't realize that no weapon form against me could ever prosper. But my heart and every attempt to get closer to God were pure and genuine and the Lord covered me with His faithfulness. It was ordained before the foundation of the world that I among millions of others would be saved. I felt his guidance and it was so obvious to me that my past would soon be behind me and my future was close at hand.

Thank God His ways are not like our ways…or His thoughts like our thoughts. He spared my life to receive a more abundant life, free from sin with the chance to experience a personal relationship with Jesus. It was a new day…and things suddenly don't look as bad as they once did. There is a scripture that says…weeping may endure for a night, but joy cometh in the morning. Psalm 30:5, troubles don't last always and situations truly are not as bad as they appear to be. The problem is that we focus too much on the problems in our lives and not on the One that is able to solve any dilemma that may challenge us.

Our inner man speaks, but we override the quiet voice with our own faulty perceptions. If we train ourselves to be still and listen, in our silent moments we will discover peace and the word to comfort us to a place of safety. Your natural thinking process is highly important, but a renewed mind led by the spirit makes all the difference. Your decisions and reactions rest upon the response of the state of your mind, and the information inside of you that will qualify your decision. If you have the mind of Christ you can be led by the Spirit of Christ. Your mental thinking capacity can only take you so far, you are limited, based on what you know and think. But if you are a new creature in Christ and have been born again with your sins washed away and forgiven; and filled with the Spirit of God, which is the Holy Ghost you can be led into all truth. Diligently seek Him. There are many changes that I have experienced since I have been saved. There are so many benefits and rewards, knowing that you have Jesus to lead and guide you.

Prayer is the key and is essential in your relationship with the Lord. Prayer allows us to be personal with God and we can be as close and as intimate with the Lord as our hearts desire. I willingly started to talk with the Lord, not fully understanding all of what I was doing at the time. The Lord was with me and He was about to accomplish a mighty work within me. My spiritual appetite was hungry. I wanted to be filled. I could feel the love of God pulling me towards a new course in life. It was a miracle in action and the scripture in John 6:44 that says, no man can come to me, except the Father which hath sent me draw him: and I will raise him up at the last day. This scripture became alive in my life and was a real true experience.

I was moving towards God…it was not my doing or abilities, but my heart was obedient and my motives and desires were established within me to reach Him. I was striving with everything I had to complete my salvation according to the scriptures. I began to attend church once again on a regular basis and the Word stayed with me. The more I heard, the more I wanted. The word was very much, a live word. It repeated itself inside of me over and over…it demanded an answer… it found me in my situation and began to deal with me at my level in understanding. The Word found me guilty and in need of a saviour. The word was a mirror and I saw myself empty and naked before the Lord. I was nothing of worth in this condition. I knew it was time to repent and give my life to Jesus. I knew this for some time. Once I presented myself before the Lord it was going to be up to Him to move all mountains in my way and I turned the entire situation over to Him. It was ordained for a specific time and my salvation would be no accident.

It was on a glorious Thursday night that I decided to be baptized. A telephone call was placed to the assistance pastor and arrangements were made for me to be baptized. I didn't have transportation at that time and some of the ministers arrived to take me to church. On the way to the church the car that we were all riding in was operating fine and then suddenly… the car stopped for no apparent reason. One of the ministers made the remark that this was just like the devil…I looked around in dismay, wondering where was the devil and what power did he have over my decision to get baptized. I didn't know how determined he was to stop the plan of God. But I believed in the report of the Lord. Jesus is greater and much more powerful, He is in control of everything that exist. God created the evil one. There is nothing to hard for the Lord and His arm is not short that He cannot save. I knew I was in good hands!!! God had taken care of me this far. Upon examining the car it had a flat tire, one of the brothers started to fix it as the others began to "plead the blood of Jesus," believing that Satan was behind the delay. It was taking to long, I was getting anxious. Then questions of doubt and fear rushed into my mind, should I get baptized or not...was it really worth all this? Then I got afraid because it was like a vivid conversation with the devil started taking place, he was telling me, "look at you out here in the night, going to church to get baptized, and here you are stranded on the side of the road...it's your fault, you have all these good people doing all of this for you...then the devil said, it doesn't matter because if you get baptized you're going to die anyway because you can't swim and you will surely die in the water!!! Now what??? The picture was painted and the seed of destruction was planted. Now what was I going to do? These good people had went out of their way to assist me in my decision to get baptized...but it was true...I could not swim...what would I do?

Finally, we arrived at church. Many other saints had also gathered for the baptism. They were singing songs and rejoicing. They rushed me to the dressing room to prepare for the watery death. I really didn't know the devil, but he was making himself more acquainted with me as the minutes went on. God, where was my faith? Where was my power? The enemy continued to say, "you can't swim, if you get baptized you are going to drown!!!" I began to panic. I heard the devil say, "change your mind and save your life..." And then I heard my inner spirit say, "go ahead...everything will be all right, have no fear for I am with you!!!" And suddenly, I moved away from fear and trusted in God, believing that everything would be all right. I moved in obedience and embraced the love of God and repented of all my sins and cried out to be saved and forgiven for the delay in my faith. Now, I was ready to accept Jesus as the head of my life and at that point I was ready for baptism.

Everything was ready and the Honorable Elder Everett Farmer, now of Tennessee baptized me in The Name of Jesus Christ for the remission of my sins. It was awesome...as He baptized me, He didn't cover my nose...He pronounced the authority of Jesus Name over me and laid me down in the water and I seem to have floated for several minutes, it was a measure of time...I felt light in body weight and I could see clearly...I had my eyes open!!! I saw lights and my past was being washed away and I got lighter in weight under the water and it seemed as if I went back to my childhood and a innocence swept over me and I died to sin that night and was accepted in the Beloved, my Lord and Savior Jesus Christ!!! I was clean as snow and my record was clean. My sins were washed away by the blood of Jesus.

That night I rejoiced in the God of my salvation. The Lord had blessed me to be baptized and the empty feeling was gone. I quickly felt peace and was covered in the security of God's word. I had the best sleep I could remember. I slept like a newborn baby without a care in the world. I was so thankful, I had been washed in the blood of the lamb and there was no condemnation. Then I started to think about the fact that I needed the Holy Ghost...The Heavens rejoice with praise when one soul is added to the kingdom. It was time for me to complete my spiritual birth!!!

CHAPTER 8
KNOW YOUR DESTINY

He came to do the will of his father.

In the book of Luke 2:41-52 this is recorded…Now his parents went to Jerusalem every year at the feast of the Passover. And when he was twelve years old, they went up to Jerusalem after the custom of the feast. And when they had fulfilled the days, as they returned, the child Jesus tarried behind in Jerusalem; and Joseph and his mother knew not of it. But they, supposing him to have been in the company, went a day's journey; and they sought him among their kinsfolk and acquaintance. And when they found him not, they turned back again to Jerusalem, seeking him. And it came to pass, that after three days they found him in the temple, sitting in the midst of the doctors, both hearing them and asking them questions. And all that heard him were astonished at his understanding and answers. And when they saw him, they were amazed: and his mother said unto him, Son, why hast thou thus dealth with us? Behold, thy father and I have sought thee sorrowing. And he said unto them, How is it that ye sought me? Wist (In the Greek, eido, meaning: to perceive with the outward senses, understand, regard; consider) ye not that I must be about my Father's business? And they understood not the saying which he spake unto them, and came to Nazareth, and was subjected unto them: but his mother kept all these saying in her heart. And Jesus increased in wisdom and stature, and in favor with God and man.

There is another account: Luke 3:21-23. Now when all the people were baptized, it came to pass, that Jesus also being baptized, and praying, the heaven was opened. And the Holy Ghost descending in a bodily shape like a dove upon him, and a voice came from heaven, which said, Thou art my beloved Son; in thee I am well pleased. And Jesus himself began to be about thirty years of age...It is incredible how the scriptures give us this valuable information to let us know that Jesus himself was subjected to the rules of his earthly parents, he studied the law and learned what was written in the holy scribes. From the age of 12 to 30 he sought out to know the will and purpose of God. In Luke 4:18-21, the purpose of God is given and was fulfilled. The Spirit of the Lord is upon me, because he hath anointed me to preach the gospel to the poor, he hath sent me to heal the brokenhearted, to preach deliverance to the captives and recovering sight to the blind, to set at liberty them that are bruised. To preach the acceptable year of the Lord. And he closed the book, and he gave it again to the minister, and sat down. And the eyes of all them that were in the synagogue were fastened on him. And he began to say unto them, This day is the Scripture fulfilled in your ears. Jesus knew his purpose and submitted to the obedience of God so that the Fathers' will would be done on earth as it is in heaven.

Jesus always made reference to the Father. He said, I and my Father are one, I seek not mine own will, but the will of the Father that have sent me. He said many times, I am come in the name of my Father. In all things He acknowledged the Father and prayed earnestly to the Father. There was a relationship and there was true worship and obedience to God. Then God reveals through Jesus that he would go away...but he said the Comforter is come...John 15:26 says, But when the Comforter is come, whom I will send unto you from the Father, even the Spirit of truth, which proceeded from the Father, he shall testify of me. Now, let's review John 16:5-7. But now I go my way to him that sent me; and none of you asketh me, whither goest thou? But because I have said these things unto you, sorrow hath filled your heart. Nevertheless I tell you the truth; it is expedient for you that I go away: for if I go not away, the Comforter will not come unto you; but if I depart, I will send him unto you. And when he is come...verse 13...Howbeit when he, the Spirit of truth is come, he will guide you into all truth: for he shall not speak of himself; but whatsoever he shall hear, that shall he speak and he will show you things to come.

Jesus is speaking to his disciples and telling them in advance that he was going away, but he would send the Comforter. The Comforter is the Holy Ghost. It is the spirit of the living God and this Spirit would abide with us forever even unto the ends of the earth. Jesus talked to the Father and He knew what his destiny was. It was a bitter cup and he prayed that God would not forsake him and to take the cup away from him... but that was the flesh crying out. Jesus lived the will of God and his whole life was to please the father...

When you read the Book of Acts, which is the history of the church. Jesus begins to deliver a new message to his disciples about being baptized with the Holy Ghost. In Acts 1:5, For John truly baptized with water; but ye shall be baptized with the Holy Ghost not many days hence. In verse 8 it states, But ye shall receive power, after that the Holy Ghost is come upon you; and ye shall be witnesses unto me both in Jerusalem, and in all Judea, and in Samaria, and unto, the uttermost part of the earth. This power would have great potential causing them to be a witness everywhere they went. Once they received the word of the Lord, it didn't take long for it to be so...In Acts chapter 2:1-4, the promise of God is fulfilled...And when the day of Pentecost was fully come, they were all with one accord in one place, and suddenly there came a sound from heaven as a rushing mighty wind, and it filled all the house where they were sitting. And there appeared unto them cloven tongues like as of fire, and it sat upon each of them. And they were all filled with the Holy Ghost, and began to speak with other tongues, as the Spirit gave them utterance.

Now as I have given you only a few scriptures concerning the Holy Ghost and the importance of knowing your destiny, I'd also like to share the story of Nicodemus. Let's examine the scriptures. In John 3: 1- 7 it defines...There was a man of the Pharisees, named Nicodemus, a ruler of the Jews: The same came to Jesus by night, and said unto him, Rabbi (or Master), we know that thou art a teacher come from God: for no man can do these miracles that thou doest, except God be with him. Jesus answer and said unto him, Verily, verily, I say unto thee, except a man be born again, he cannot see the kingdom of God. Nicodemus saith unto him, how can a man be born when he is old? Can he enter the second time into his mother's womb, and be born? Jesus answered, Verily, Verily, I say unto thee, Except a man be born of water and of the Spirit, he cannot enter into the kingdom of God. That which is born of the flesh is flesh; and that which is born of the Spirit is spirit. Marvel not that I said unto thee, ye must be born again.

To be born of the water by baptism and born of the Spirit by the Holy Ghost completes our spiritual birth in Christ Jesus. You have faith in the Word to believe what it says and your faith will cause you to act and respond to the instructions of the Father. He left a living record that is a testament to his will and we are his inheritance. Everything the Father has promised it has already been fulfilled and accomplished in the earth. Have you received the Holy Ghost since you believed? The Holy Ghost is God dwelling on the inside of our bodies, our mind and spirit. He moves us by his Spirit. He speaks to us through his Spirit, and for certain through his word, if we can hear…what the Spirit is saying!!! We can read the word, but has the eyes of our understanding become open to receive the inspired word as truth. Are you a new creature in Christ? Born of the water and Spirit. Has your nature changed? Is the spiritual man being renewed day by day and do you have control over the fleshy nature?

The Holy Spirit is the greatest gift He has given since the breath of life. It truly is life to the soul and your spiritual man is awake unto God. You now have communion with God, true fellowship and intimacy with your heavenly Father that has prepared all things for you. You are no longer called servants, or an enemy of God, or thought of as only a friend of God. But you are a child of the Most High, and if you be lead by the Spirit of God, you are the sons of God. Romans 8:14.

The more we allow Jesus to inhabit our lives and take control, the more we will be able to walk in the Spirit. He dwells on the inside and He fills the depths of our soul, mind and emotions. The following scriptures in Romans 8:5-13 present choices: For they that are after the flesh do mind the things of the flesh, but they that are after the Spirit the things of the Spirit. For to be carnally minded is death; but to be spiritually minded is life and peace. Because the carnal mind is enmity against God, for it is not subject to the law of God, neither indeed can be. So then they that are in the flesh cannot please God. But ye are not in the flesh, but in the Spirit, if so be that the Spirit of God dwell in you. Now, if any man have not the Spirit of Christ, he is none of his. And if, Christ be in you, the body is dead because of sin; but the Spirit is life because of righteousness. But if the Spirit of him that raised up Jesus from the dead dwell in you, he that raised up Christ from the dead shall also quicken your mortal bodies by his Spirit that dwelleth in you. Therefore, brethren, we are debtors, not to the flesh, to live after the flesh. For if ye live after the flesh, ye shall die: but if ye through the Spirit do mortify the deeds of the body, ye shall live. Those scriptures mean exactly what they say. If you know anything about God...know this, He is true to His word and it is forever settled in heaven. Psalm 119: 89.

Be led by the Spirit and you shall live. Seek the Lord diligently, He will instruct you and give you the direction that you need in your life. All his ways are right and his way leads to life. If you be found in him, you will have eternal life!!! He is eternal and has no beginning or end. He wants us to have truth...not speculations of doubt. You can know Him for yourself and get just as close to him as you desire. Submit yourself in daily prayer. Take the time to listen to God speak, in the spirit, and through his word. Meditate on Him daily and commit your ways into the hands of the Lord and He will deliver you from the circumstances of life.

CHAPTER 9
SEED OF LIFE

God has placed a seed of destiny inside of us.

As it is in the natural sense so it is in the spiritual. Think on this wise, when a seed is planted in the earth to initiate growth in order for the seed to mature the seed must receive the proper nutrients to be fruitful and multiply. The nourishments are essential to the life of the seed. If the seed is not cultivated properly it may not survive and wither away in death. Every seed must grow and develop deep roots to sustain a thriving life. Spiritually, we need the Holy Ghost and we will never grow in Christ without it or be effective witnesses. What a privilege to know that Jesus is soon to return. He said to occupy, stay busy and do greater works in his name until He returns. When he returns shall he find faith in the earth…will He find faith in you? It is my prayer that if you haven't received the precious gift of the Holy Ghost you will accept Jesus into your heart and receive Him now…you don't have to wait or tarry, the gift is ready and available now. It's according to your faith and the power that is already working inside you!!!

Our very existence is only due to the Lord's mercy and grace. Just a little seed of faith that has been planted within your heart can erupt into new heights in God like never before. Be properly washed in the water of the word and you will produce more fruit. The spirit of God will give you power to overcome and become more than a conquer. God will redefine your true calling in ministry. The more He gives to you, the more you give to the kingdom of God. When you have the Holy Ghost it's easy to live for Him. You will be able to see that what the devil meant for evil, the Lord turns it around for the good. There is no weapon formed against you that shall prosper...Isaiah 54:17. He first loved us in that while we were yet sinners, Romans 5:8, But God commendeth his love towards us, in that, while we were yet sinners Christ died for us. Even in logical reasoning one could come to the conclusion that we don't deserve the goodness of Jesus!!!

Isaiah 64 says it best in the first portion of verse 6, but we are all as an unclean thing, and all our righteousness are as filthy rags...and we know that He didn't have to save us...but, so glad that He did!!! Jesus has been better to you than you have been to yourself!!! How great is God? His ways are past finding out. The unmerited favor that you don't deserve is freely given as grace.

When I received the Holy Ghost it was calling on Jesus. My soul wasn't right until I received God's spirit on the inside. After getting baptized some people had expressed that if I was truly ready...I would get the Holy Ghost coming up out of the water. But it didn't happen like that for me. In fact I was presenting myself on the altar and seeking God for the Holy Ghost as much as I could. I went through for about three months... attending neighboring churches in their "upper room." Places of prayer that were anointed with the Spirit of God where many people were receiving the Holy Ghost, Some say, you don't have to tarry...which means to wait. I'm sure you don't have to wait, if you're ready. The power to save is available now. I think my problem was my approach to God...I believed, but my surrender seemed to be hindered by my past. I knew I had repented of all my sin and I believed that I gave up everything that was not pleasing to God. But for some reason, it wasn't as easy for me as I had heard others report. I was determined and continued to pray and seek God and several times I even fasted, but every time I was told to come back and believe God!!!

I thought I had believed...but I guess, not enough. The Lord knows our heart and I was getting upset that my sincerity had not moved God. What was it? Did I sin along the way...was something wrong with the condition of my heart or attitude? I didn't feel condemned by anything and felt I was right to come before his presence...so I pressed on and one day at home in prayer I got encouraged and I decided in my mind I was going to get the Holy Ghost. As I worshipped God at home my spirit was feeling stronger, but I was a babe in Christ and there was so much I didn't know...this particular night at church I went forth like it was the last time and I could sense within myself I was getting closer...to receiving. Every time I thought I was about to touch the hem of his garment...I would start to choke and cough and swallow. I was thirsty and tired emotionally from crying and at the same time, trying to elevate my mind and concentrate on God. I was working to hard...but I didn't stop!!! I held my arms up in worship and I could hear the music and people whispering in my ear and then suddenly, it didn't matter and tears began to flow...I was gone into another realm and all I could see in my mind was Jesus on the cross and He was high...high and lift up.

I started to call on Jesus, on bended knees I continued to call on Jesus and in my mind I was saying that I was sorry for the sins that I had committed against Him. As I said the Name of Jesus, it went into...thank you Jesus...I was surrendering my will and Jesus was receiving my cry. My language began to change and I went into stammering lips...and the stammering lips went into praising God in a heavenly language. I had no control of my tongue and I didn't know what I was saying. I was in the room physically, but it seemed as if I was far in the heavens on a clear blue and sunny day and nobody was present, only Jesus and me. Then, to hear myself speak this language and I could hear the singing and the rejoicing around me, and yet feel far away...something came over me and I stopped. I came back to myself and opened my eyes...I just stopped. I felt dizzy and not quite sure of what had taken place. Nobody said a word. I didn't say very much either, except for, "thank you Jesus!!!" There were a few people at church that night that received the Holy Ghost. They came up to the front and shouted out to everyone as a way of broadcasting the good news, "I got the Holy Ghost!!!" I sat in my seat wondering, if I had gotten it or not...the experience didn't last long enough, so I decided to wait...

People started telling me that they would pray for me...next time...you were so close!!! No I was fooled by the enemy!!! I did not believe that I had received the Holy Ghost!!! But according to scripture I did speak, and I did receive, but my human intellect got in the way and the devil seized the moment. Later, after thinking about what happen, I knew I got it...I knew I had received it and the Lord would confirm it and let me speak again. My time and chance came again, and I spoke in a unknown tongue until the joy of the Lord was in my spirit...I had received the precious gift of the Holy Ghost and now my spiritual birth was complete, this all happened in November of 1979, before Thanksgiving Day.

CHAPTER 10
LIVE TO WIN

*Remember, only what you do for Christ will last and will be
counted at the end!!!*

Once you are in Christ, your life is not your own!!!
Think about it, for an example: when a very famous
movie star or celebrity stands before God...and if they
have not reconciled their life to Christ...can you picture
the topic of discussion? The Lord will demand an
answer concerning what they have did with their life.
What did they accomplish for Christ with the talents
and abilities He invested in them...did they win souls
for the Lord in any of their winning performances?
Because of their position was their voice heard for the
right appeal instead of the wrong cause? Did their rich
lifestyle contribute to the kingdom of God...Will their
celebrity status earn them jewels in their crown of
righteousness, will there be honor or dishonor within
their gates?

The Lord will be the only one giving out the
rewards...and the history of a persons' life is being
written now, today. Only what you do for Christ will
matter in the end and whatever you have done with
the life He gives you...you will be the only one that

stands up before God, for yourself. The scripture tells us that, every one of us shall give account of himself to God. Romans 14:12.

We only have today. We need to be busy about our Fathers' business. We are living in perilous times... dangerous and changing times. In Matthew 9:37 & 38 the scriptures states, then saith he unto his disciples, The harvest truly is plenteous, but the laborers are few; Pray ye therefore the Lord of the harvest, that he will send forth laborers into his harvest. The reason for this is plainly stated in Jeremiah 8:20, The harvest is past, the summer is ended, and we still are not saved!!! God wants to save souls. He is made rich when souls are added to the kingdom of God!!! He died for not some of us, but for ALL mankind. To as many that shall receive Him and to as many that will believe on his name.

In St. John 4:35-38 it reads, Say not ye, There are yet four months; and then cometh harvest? Behold, I say unto you, Lift up your eyes, and look on the fields, for they are white already to harvest. And he that reapeth receiveth wages, and gathereth fruit unto life eternal: that both he that soweth and he that reapeth may rejoice together. And herein is that saying true, One soweth, and another reapeth. I sent you to reap that whereon ye bestowed no labor; other men labored, and ye are entered into their labors. I am tied to someone else and I must have a part in helping souls to be saved!!! It is a duty and a obligation that every Christian should be a witness for Christ, and I Peter 3:15 says, But sanctify the Lord God in your hearts: and be ready always to give an answer to every man that asketh you a reason of the hope that is in you with meekness and fear. We can't live to simply satisfy ourselves, but rather to please God in our lives and service to Him.

We must always examine ourselves, to be sure that our lives line up with the word of God. The word is a guide to show us our sins and short comings, as well as to give us the reflections of what we will be as we become more like Christ. Each person is responsible to judge himself and when you stand before God, you will stand for yourself and give an account to God for the deeds done in your body. Ecclesiastes 12:13 and verse 14 says, Let us hear the conclusion of the whole matter: Fear God, and keep his commandments: for this is the whole duty of man. For God shall bring every work into judgment, with every secret thing, whether it be good or whether it be evil.

Now is the time to repent. This is the day of salvation and deliverance. This is the day of hope, now is the time to call on Jesus. Tomorrow is not promised, we have been given the light of the glorious gospel, today. Every soul belongs to God and we will be accountable for the life we have chosen to live and the decisions we made. In this life you will have had an exceptional opportunities to hear the gospel of Jesus Christ. It will be your choice to repent of your sins and to accept, believe or even reject the salvation of Jesus Christ. You can choose to become a saint of The Most High God and receive his spirit, which is the Holy Ghost. Your life will testify for you or against you and it will bear true witness. God is recording your life and you will be judged out of the books...in Revelation

20:12-15 it describes the final judgment day, And I saw the dead, small and great, stand before God; and the books were opened: and another book was opened, which is the book of life; and the dead were judged out of those things which were written in the books, according to their works. And the sea gave up the dead which were in it; and death and hell delivered up the dead which were in them: and they were judged every man according to their works. And death and hell were cast into the lake of fire. This is the second death. And whosoever was not found written in the book of life was cast into the lake of fire. Trust God and keep his commandments!!! Hell is a place of torment and you don't want to be sent there, it's only temporary like a "holding cell," until the final judgment has been pronounced. The lake of fire is final!!! Once you get there…it is no way out!!! No back door, no front door, and no sliding entrance. You are locked in and you will burn with fire and brimstone, in a fire that is never quenched…it will burn forever and ever. Jesus holds the keys to life and death.

Take note, you are being judged according to your works, and your deeds whether good or evil. You are sending yourself to a place of eternal damnation. Everlasting punishment!!! If your name is not written in the book of life your sentence will be a profound announcement, and God will sit on the throne as the supreme judge. His word will be final. It's something to think about because you have had a lifetime to accept a loving Saviour, one that was willing to die for our sins and He knew no sin…but his love paid the price so that we would not have to face death, and the penalties of sin, but chose life. Jesus prepared the way.

If you happen to go to Hell...this temporary holding cell is available for you while you await your pending trial and your actual sentencing...but when your judgment is rendered based on the true facts of your life...death and hell shall meet...and so shall you every spend eternity cast into the lake of fire. The Book of Revelation 20: 12-15 reads like this: And I saw the dead, small and great, stand before God; and the books were opened: and another book was opened, which is the book of life: and the dead were judged out of those things which were written in the books, according to their works. And the sea gave up the dead which were in it; and death and hell delivered up the dead which were in them: and they were judged every man according to their works. And death and hell were cast into the lake of fire. This is the second death. And whosoever was not found written in the book of life was cast into the lake of fire.

Do not reject God when His love is reaching out to save you. Invest in your life, it is the best commitment you will every make!!! Your soul depends upon it!!! Give some of your precious time and your hard work to the kingdom of God. Remember only what you do for Christ shall last and that will make the difference in the end. The sacrifices we make today will mean much more tomorrow, the very cost of what we pay will have a value that far exceeds our human understanding. The returns can work either way!!! It's always based on what you put in...so I invite you to invest in your life. Your soul is the only thing you own value it.

In the Book of Revelations 22:12 and 13 it says, "And behold, I come quickly; and my reward is with me, to give every man according as his work shall be. I am Alpha and Omega, the beginning and the end, the first and the last." And verse 14 is what it is all about... Blessed are they that do his commandments, that they may have a right to the tree of life and may enter in through the gates into the city. It is my prayer that we purpose in our hearts to live for Jesus. There is a city called Heaven, being prepared with you in mind. It's a city for a prepared people whose maker and builder is God!!! Don't you want to go? We travel the world over and make all types of preparations to have a great and wonderful trip. Do you want to go where your soul can find rest? Heaven is the City and only Jesus can take you there. But you need to make reservations early and in advance, have your ticket ready, this flight will be a super take off... quick and in the blinking of an eye, scheduled to leave at anytime...

In Revelation 21:3-5 we can comfort one another with these words: And I heard a great voice out of heaven saying, Behold, the tabernacle of God is with men, and he will dwell with them, and they shall be his people, and God himself shall be with them, and be their God. And God shall wipe away all tears from their eyes; and there shall be no more death, neither sorrow, nor crying, neither shall there be any more pain: for the former things are passed away. And he that sat upon the throne said, Behold, I make all things new. And he said unto me, Write: for these words are true and faithful. And he said unto me, It is done, I am Alpha and Omega, the beginning and the end. I will give unto him that is athrist of the fountain of the water of life freely. He that overcometh shall inherit all things; and I will be his God, and he shall be my son.

But the fearful, and unbelieving, and the abominable, and murderers, and whoremongers, and sorcerers, and idolaters, and all liars, shall have their part in the lake which burneth with fire and brimstone: which is the second death. Let us hear the conclusion of the whole matter: Fear God, and keep his commandments: For this is the whole duty of man. Ecclesiastes 12:13.

CHAPTER 11
REAP ETERNAL LIFE

You can only get what you plant in your life.

If you sow to the spirit, you can reap everlasting life. Whatsoever a man soweth, that shall he also reap. For he that soweth to his flesh shall of the flesh reap corruption; but he that soweth to the Spirit shall of the Spirit reap life everlasting. (Galatians 6:7 & 8) We have our lifetime to consciously and intellectually decide how we will live our lives. All the choices we make today will affect decisions for tomorrow. If we live a godly life, the scripture tells us that in due season we shall reap, if we faint not. (Galatians 6: 9). The Bible also tells us that the wages of sin is death, which is the payday for the penalties of your transgressions. Although we don't like to think in those terms it's our own decisions and willful disobedience that puts us in opposition to God.

We must plant the right seeds in our lives. As a born-again Christian, we should be planting seeds of righteousness. The outward appearance is always judged first by the standards of people, but the inward man, the soul of a man is inherited by the Spirit of the living God and He judges that which is within. We should renew ourselves day by day. What you may or may not be planting on the inside of your mind and heart can defile or destroy you. The seed of faith and righteousness can edify and build you up. Sowing and reaping is a principle of God.

We should plant good virtues that will produce more favor with God and man. Shaping our character with the word of God will cause us to be more like Christ and less concerned with our "ego" self, the pride of life and attitudes that stunt our spiritual growth. This generation is one that has an appetite for the things of the world and the pleasures of the day. The fleshly man or carnal man has no control over his desires and wants. His extreme cravings will take him to places of no return. Where the flesh is never satisfied or quenched. The flesh and the spirit have always been in opposition and a real battle takes place in the mind to prevail one against the other. If the spirit is weak, that person will reap more to the flesh. But if the spirit is strong, that person is strong in the faith and will sow to the spirit and will reap an abundant life. Your flesh will never go to Heaven…it has already been ordained to return back to the dust of the earth when you depart this life. But if you sow to the spirit you shall live and have eternal life.

You can never get close to God when your flesh stands in the way. God hates pride!!! The carnal man does not have the mind of God and is not concerned about the things of God. His thinking is far away from God and all that remains to be seen or heard is, me… myself and I!!! So much pride, no earthly good. The scriptures in Romans 8 verses 5 through 8 reads as follows: For they that are after the flesh do mind the things of the flesh; but they that are after the Spirit the things of the Spirit. For to be carnally minded is death, but to be spiritually minded is life and peace. Because the carnal mind is enmity against God, it is not subject to the law of God, neither indeed can be. So then they that are in the flesh cannot please God. We need to examine ourselves. Judge if you are in the faith!!! Seek God and review what we are permitting to get into our spirits. Our lifestyles and personal relationships may not necessarily be acceptable to the Father. The Lord is seeking for true worshippers and they that worship him…must worship in spirit and in truth!!! St John 4: 24. How can a carnal man worship? His heart and soul is not dedicated to God and his flesh is not alive unto God, He only participates for self- gratification, deceit and vain glory.

But ye are not in the flesh, but in the Spirit, if so be that the Spirit of God dwell in you. Now if any man have not the Spirit of Christ, he is none of his. Romans 8:9!!! Here lies one of the most important details in the scriptures…IF SO BE THAT THE SPIRIT OF GOD DWELL IN YOU!!! With God inside you…you have the answer to any and all problems in your life. The very spirit of God, that abides inside of you, which is the Holy Spirit, also called the Holy Ghost throughout the Bible supplies you with all hope, all faith; and all strength in weakness that you will ever need. You were created by God in his image and likeness. You have authority, dominion and power. In Genesis 1:26-28 it states, And God said, Let us make man in our image, after our likeness; and let them have dominion over the fish of the sea, and over the fowl of the air, and over the cattle, and over all the earth, and over every creeping thing that creepeth upon the earth. So God created man in his own image, in the image of God created he him, male and female created he them. And God blessed them, and God said unto them, Be fruitful, and multiply, and replenish the earth, and subdue it; and have dominion over the fish of the sea, and over the fowl of the air, and over every living thing that moveth upon the earth.

You are to rule and reign while you are on planet earth!!! You are the child of the most High God, no longer are we servants...we now have ownership in the kingdom of God. You are an heir and joint heir and made righteous by the blood of Jesus Christ. Jesus now calls us sons and daughters!!! We have eternal life, now!!! There is nothing impossible with God. He can do all things perfect. There is no failure in Him. It's a matter of, do you believe; do you have the God-kind of faith to move mountains in your life? Be a mountain mover and use the power that God gave you...speak to the mountain... declare that all your needs are met. Speak to your situation by confessing the word of God. Open your Bible and study the word of God and He will open the scriptures that your understanding will be enlighten and you obtain the victory over your circumstances...speak in faith and declare; stand still and you will see the salvation of the Lord. THE ANSWER IS ON THE INSIDE...but you must sow to the spirit and submit to God.

Every Christian should live to please God. To have a holy life dedicated to live for the Lord and to die in the service of the Lord. Remembering, that you are not in the flesh, but in the spirit, if so be that the spirit of God dwells in you...you are more than a conqueror equipped to win the battle and war. The scripture tells us in II Peter1:3 that, According as his divine power hath given unto us all things that pertain unto life and godliness through the knowledge of him that hath called us to glory and virtue...we can make it. Keep His commandments and love Him with all your heart. Have charity and let the love of Jesus fill you beyond human comprehension. The mind thinks that it knows...but the heart feels and is the seat of affections. It is the heart that recognizes that we were once a sinner and later the mind is given the information as to why... these are the deep things of God and His mysteries belong to us. (Deuteronomy 29:29). The secret things belong unto the Lord our God: but those things which are revealed belong unto us and to our children forever, that we may do all the words of this law.

CHAPTER 12
JESUS IS THE LOVER OF YOUR SOUL

To know Him…is to love Him!!! He first…loved you!!!

There is no greater love, than the love of Jesus Christ for all mankind. Each one of us will have the opportunity to discover this great love for ourselves. Take it personal and seek after Jesus for your own experience. He first loved you…He was moved to actively demonstrate just how much He cared. Born to die, that you and I might live!!! He gave everything to make eternal life possible. Are we truly worthy of such a display of affection? The love of Jesus could see beyond our faults and even the angels desire to know what is it in man that God is so mindful of Him?

We were born sinners into this world and God hates sin. All unrighteousness is sin and sin will cause separation from the very presence and fellowship with God. No sin will EVER enter Heaven!!! Because of the fall of Adam, sin entered into the world and all men and women would pass through this judgment of being pronounced a sinner at the time of conception, even before we were born. We were yet sinners. The

Lord made a way of escape for you and me to be saved, to believe and receive Him in our hearts and lives. Colossians 1:12-14 gives this report: Giving thanks unto the Father, which hath made us meet (or able) to be partakers of the inheritance of the saints in light: Who hath delivered us from the power of darkness, and hath translated us into the kingdom of his dear Son: In whom we have redemption through his blood, even the forgiveness of sins. Even when we were without Christ, He died for the ungodly. He first…loved you!!!

For many, our lives have been a life of ungodliness. He draws us unto Himself. Nobody gets the first move on God. He is preeminent in all things. He puts the thought, the ability and his faith inside of us. He will meet you in your lowest state and is well able to deliver us from the hand of the enemy. His time is the right time. He is never late or in a hurry, be patient with God he is not through with you yet!!! He knows the outcome and end result of everything that exists. But time and chance happens to us all…God grants every person an opportunity to hear the Gospel and to obey. God has a set time…a now time and due season… He spoke and time came into existence. Time belongs to God and He orders your steps and will lead, if you will follow.

The Lord is standing at the door of your heart, knocking…waiting for the proper entrance as you welcome Him into your life. You say that you want to be loved…you want to share your life and give of yourself. You promised to love with every fiber within you…but where did all the love go? Why do you feel so empty this time? What has occurred that makes this time so unusual and you can feel a deep hurt that you can't seem to shake. When you have tried everything in life that you think will make you happy and you arrive at a place of predetermined success, why then do you feel empty? Why is it that you feel unworthy to have Jesus Christ as the head of your life? Why have you rejected the greatest love you could ever receive, with no strings attached. God's love is freely given... no charge!!! Why is it so hard for you to believe that Jesus is real and His word is true?

It's not in man to do what is right...a person may think he knows...but in reality, we don't. In Proverbs 20:24, it says Man's goings are of the Lord; how can a man then understand his own way? So many times we must learn the hard way, over and over again!!! Look at the time we have wasted, which could have been used to make meaningful accomplishments for the kingdom of God. Time is moving on and it waits for no one, we just keep getting older, but never wiser. Our wasted time should produced experience from our troubles, but we neglect to examine the warning signs until it's too later and then we are in trouble. God's time is really never wasted. He prepares us for our future even when we don't realize it. His glorious light is shining on us and He will lead us in the path of righteousness, yes...for his name's sake. He promised to lead us through the valley of the shadow of death... if you will repent of all your sin and accept the Lord Jesus Christ into your life at this very moment...God is ready to do everything that He has promised. You have a divine appointment and it's marked on a specific day and moment in time.

Each one of us will come to the cross roads in life. Where the two roads will meet and you are faced with the decision of your life...as you decide to accept or cancel your rendezvous with God, realize He first loved you!!! He suffered for our transgressions, sin and shame. Be obedient to the spirit of God that is now pulling you. Receive Jesus now. There is no greater love than that of Jesus Christ. John 3:16, put it this way...For God so loved the world (mankind), that he gave his only begotten Son, that whosoever believeth in him should not perish, but have everlasting life. Eternity is much longer than any given lifetime. You decide where you will spend it. It is your choice. God instructs that you choose life...that you may live and have good success and that your days may be long upon this land. Even your children...and their children shall be blessed. Keep his commandments that you may live and multiply. Worship God and live for he is your life and the length of your days. (Read Deuteronomy 30:15-20)

There must be some intimacy, some private moments in his presence, with obedience and sacrifice. You must stay in the spirit, and don't walk in the flesh. Sing songs and make melody in your heart to God and you will develop a personal relationship with the Lord that will cause you to commune daily and on purpose...because you need the Lord and can do nothing of yourself, you will be established in the faithfulness of Jesus. Your love will get sweeter and sweeter as the days go by and you will know, that He loved you best!!!

CHAPTER 13
BELIEVE

Have faith in God!!!

Be dedicated to live for Jesus, as a Christian you represent him. Trust in the Word of God to the point that you pattern your life as the word is written. Find yourself in the scriptures and know with all confidence that Jesus has you in mind and intends to do you good. He knows all about you and every detail of your life. Appreciate the Lord for His wonderful works and all the benefits you enjoy. When daily fellowship with the Lord increases, strive to know more about the Lord, seek to do His will and not all of your will, set your affections on things above, give more…and more will be given unto you. Let love and joy abound that you will always bear fruit for the kingdom.

Enter into a new realm with God. Speak to God in a heavenly language and let the spirit have its' way. The Holy Ghost or also called the Holy Spirit will make intercession for others through you, as you are directed by the Spirit. Prepare to seek God with your "whole heart and spirit". Take into account the attitude of Adam and Abraham, how they talked and communicated with God. It was a two-way voiced dialog and we called such related conversation, prayer!!! They both prayed to God and they talked to the Lord so much, they recognized his voice and knew when they were in the presence of a Holy God. When God called...they answered, they knew the voice of God. When you do have a close relationship with someone, you can instantly identify who the person is... simply by the voice.

I have learned that as you hear God speak to you, more obedience will be necessary and once you decide that it pleases the Lord to obey his voice, it is easier to simply say yes, to the Lord. It's too hard to kick against the prick!!! If you love him you will keep his word. In the lives of such men like Moses, and Abraham and Paul, God used them and they were commanded to do whatever...God said to them. God spoke and they had to submit to the will of God. God spoke commands that caused a response from each of them!!! God will take us step by step and little by little. He gives us just enough information and even provides faith. When he commands, he waits for our obedience. He waits for your free will to accept or reject his laws and statues and commandments.

For example: Adam heard the voice of God... relationship had already been previously established in Genesis 2. Adam had great ability and power. His knowledge was such that God assigned him the responsibility in Gen. 2:19 to name every living creature. He was filled with intellect. God knows what inside and He created Adam and knew his characteristics and abilities. Now, Adam sins...he was wise to the cunning type beast that the snake was, after all He named the snake...he had to know what was in the snake to call him a snake!!! To provoke further thought; he did not protect his family. The opportunity for the enemy to get in was open and the serpent seized the chance to plant the seed of doubt and sin. Eve gave place to the devil and allowed deceit to fill her heart. The fruit was pleasing to the eye and it attracted her...she was drawn to that which was not permitted. Think for a moment...Adam was the spiritual leader and provider of the family, the laws and commands that God gave was to Adam. Eve knew and heard and was very aware of what God had said and yet she made a decision against the command of God...she took of the fruit. In Genesis 3:2 and 3 she herself repeats portions of the law...And the woman said unto the serpent, We may eat of the fruit of the trees of the garden: But of the fruit of the tree which is in the midst of the garden, God hath said, Ye shall not eat of it, neither shall ye touch it, lest ye die. She even added...neither shall ye touch it...But God said...thou shalt not eat of it: for in the day that thou eatest thereof thou shall surely die.

God placed Adam as the head and leader of the family. Eve was made from the rib and Adam said... (remember the power and ability to know is within him) This is now bone of my bones, and flesh of my flesh: and she shall be called Woman, because she was taken out of Man. (Gen. 2:23). Adam called it because dominion, and power was placed in him and the commandments were given to Him. In his position towards God he fell short. His disobedience...was sinful and no excuse was worthy of an answer.

He lived in the presence of God and was intimate with God and knew his voice. Now, sin enters and separates the fellowship between man and God. Judgment is passed upon the whole human race. Sin has a price to be paid and when man fell because of his sin, spiritual death took place!!! Satan lied when he told Eve, that she would not surely die...no, she didn't die physically that day...but a spiritual death sentence was upon them both and only the blood of Jesus could repay the debt of sin. Sin has a price and for far to many it has cost their lives. Jesus gave his life that we would be free and today His blood still covers us and keeps us under His banner of love. Believe God and keep his commandments.

CHAPTER 14
MORNING DREAM

While dreams just don't occur at night…miracles come early!!!

On one Sunday morning in March of 2002, I was called out of sleep and at the time; what I thought was a bad dream, seem to linger fresh before me. As I began to come to myself and totally realizing that I clearly understood what had just taken place, I knew at this moment it was not meant to be explained in my thought process as a bad dream, but rather to accept the fact that God had given me divine revelation for the answers in my distant future.

Often times we seldom even think about what we dream. But instantly reject the unusual and unpleasant events as we awake and recall these memories, as a bad dream. But I discovered that the circumstances surrounding our lives can be contained in the resources of dreams. As we sleep, our mind is busy processing information that is being stored as hidden data. God provides us with many avenues in which he can speak. The Lord can choose any method He desires to deal with us to get his will accomplished in the earth. If we say that we have a personal relationship with God, and live a life free from sin and daily have communion and fellowship with man and God, through our intimacy and love for the Lord, our heavenly Father can anoint, direct and lead us to do his will with power and personal conviction. He will reveal truth...and it is truth that will deliver your soul unto salvation.

My sleep was gone... I suddenly emerged into a fast pace awakening and the spiritual knowledge was forth coming and very quick. It was necessary to speak aloud to my husband in order to record in my memory what I had experienced. I was able to see myself...as if it was actually happening at that moment. It was like looking at a movie with live dramatic action. The thoughts of the dream carried me into a replay, a temporary vision in vivid details. I became vocal and began to express what I had seen. I attempted to articulate what I first thought was bad, at first it was unexplainable and didn't make sense to me...but then I found myself in the Spirit...on the Lord's day and it was clear that I couldn't keep it to myself. I made sure my husband was a witness to this miracle and commenced to share the mysteries that had been revealed to me!!! It was an awesome display of Gods' love. His presence was so close. His presence was in me, even in my mouth. I must confess, there is none like God!!! There were no burdens upon me, no sickness or pain. His anointing was upon me and I was caught in the spirit of counsel and revelation knowledge. This had never happen to me before!!!

On that day I had Gods' strength and all fear was gone, there was no doubt and I was not afraid...only willing to submit to this great and mighty God that had so sweetly demonstrated yet again His Love. To discover the wisdom that had been manifested within me was so exciting. His truth gives light to our understanding and the entrance of my soul had received all that God wanted me to do, next!!! There are so many issues that we don't have answers for, but this revelation provided the answers that made sense. I was able to accept and believe that what God was doing at that precise moment was showing me the difficult season in my life and what it meant. It truly was miraculous. I responded in praise and thanksgiving for the deliverance to receive victory in my life. The seed was planted inside of me. The roots of life soon would spring forth, providing everlasting hope. It was a glorious day, a miracle come early.

Now...back to the dream!!! I was in a big city. I can't tell you what city, but in recent years I had plans to relocate to Atlanta, Georgia. So visualize with me a city of that magnitude. I could see the skyscrapers everywhere. I could see automobiles in traffic and hear the noise of a nearby super highway. There were a multitude of sounds, coming from every direction. It was hot and I seem to be in the middle of a downtown heat wave. We were walking in the heat of the day...

I was with two other ladies that appeared to be younger than myself. We had just shared lunch together and we were coming out of a family style restaurant. The two young ladies were talking more to each other and carried themselves like they were close friends. They were engaged in conversation and I seemed to be focused on something else. They were laughing and one was looking for something in her handbag...in a brief moment, we all seemed to be standing still in front of the diner, like in a freeze mode. I looked up and in full view was this city. It was if I was on a top pinnacle and could see everything above and around it. Then, suddenly...I felt the effects of a great and ferocious wind. I called out loudly to the ladies... but it appeared that they were not affected by the impending danger. They were busy and preoccupied and didn't observe their surroundings. They didn't seem to care. I tried to warn them that danger was approaching. I wanted them to see what was coming, when I got their attention, and they began to see for themselves they were paralyzed and could not move for fear!!! They were huddled together and began to scream and cry. I stood alone, but yet seem to have a force of an army with me. I had hoped the young ladies could intervene in prayer with me, but they were defeated by the threat of danger, not prepared to fight against it!!!

I saw world winds before me...enormous funnel clouds similar to that of a hurricane. From a great distance...I saw three separate raging winds, blowing and spinning around with lighting flashing and heavy rains pouring...but not directly upon us!!! The air was extremely hot and then cool... the sky was dark and I could feel the presence of an unpredictable storm. In a slow moving pace one of the funnels began to advance, turning slowly. The wind in the middle was largest and had the greatest force, it stayed in its' place moving with a sound of a train that had roaring speed. Then yet, the smallest of the group was actually getting closer; but it could not get as close as it wanted...something was holding it back and yet it continued to push it's way forward, but it was not able to reach us. I began to rebuke the winds in Jesus name...I demanded and commanded by the power that had been invested in me that the destructive force behind the winds would not prevail and no harm would come to any of us. I sparing no mercy, rebuked the winds. The presence of God was with me!!! I was speaking to the winds in an unknown tongue and the rage of the winds decreased and retreated back until all three vanished in the air.

And suddenly...the winds were gone!!! I saw myself moving in the power of God...the young ladies were on the ground and seem to be crying for God. I extended comfort to them and prayed that the will of God be done in their lives. There was lack of faith in them and they were afraid. We must always have faith in God, so that His perfect will can be done in us. God cannot and will not operate when there is a lack of faith in Him. With faith, He will move every mountain and do the unexpected in victory every time!!!

CHAPTER 15
BE STILL…AND KNOW!!!

God Will Reveal in His Own Time. He Alone Is God!!!

The Lord revealed that storms always mean trouble and approaching danger in your life. The winds of terror were meant to destroy me and each represented troubling issues and pain and fears which were attempting to break my will and covenant relationship with God. My determination and trust are a part of who I am, but my commitment to serve him had been cut off…I never stopped praying and always communicated with God. What the devil meant for evil, God turned it around for good. The enemy had plans to divide my natural family and also separate me from my spiritual house of worship. But the house that God builds is a building not made with hands, but eternal in the heavens. This house that God builds no man can destroy and satan forgot that the gates of hell can't prevail against it!!! I am the church of the living God and the Church is in me…not a physical building that is ordained as the place of worship!!! From this maneuver the enemy desired to destroy my family and the love we all hold dear for the church.

I have always loved church from a young girl 10 years old. I served with the love of God in my heart and prayed that whatever I offered would be acceptable to God and the saints. The enemy has a plan to try and kill what God has created. The devil is mad. He is bound. He will never ever abide in Heaven. But you and I have a right to an abundant life here and now and to live throughout eternity in the presence of God. Wherever He is... there shall we be with Him, forever. The Lord gave me deliverance and victory over everyone and everything that was represented in the dream.

We have the power and ability to speak to the storms and winds in our lives and say just like Jesus said... "Peace be still!!!" I have matured as a Christian and deal with my problems in a God instructed way. I inquire of the Lord early in the morning. I make a daily sacrifice to offer the best time to God in prayer. During this period in my life, I was in constant prayer!!! I was calling upon the Lord as the spirit was leading...I continued in prayer and I talked with God and listened to what the Spirit had to say to me. I stayed in the Word and I found myself very often in the spirit. The more I filled myself with the Word, the stronger I got. It's all written in The Bible, if we will take the time and effort and comprehend what God is saying. When we allow God to be so much the more apart of our lives. I live as a worshipper. He will intervene and dispense His divine favor when he is ready. God will bless us daily, if we will spend time with Him. My heavenly Father has said, that anything...that I ask in the name of Jesus is done!!! I love the name of Jesus and got saved and delivered from sin...calling upon the mighty name of Jesus. He has a plan for me and has said to go forth,

I'm with you!!! He has ordered my steps and He speaks and I obey.

Many are the afflictions of the righteous: but the Lord delivereth him out of them all. Psalm 34:19. He can reveal in a moment and give new life and new hope. Swift transitions are happening everyday and seemingly there is no stability. The world is filled with grief and sorrow and God is still calling for you to come to Him. In Him is peace and love. In Him is life and that everlasting. He will always love His people and nothing can separate us from the love of God. The dream that I lived, helped me to recognize; that God was allowing me to see...the days ahead of me, the time to come in my life...a new day, a better day...this day!!! I would still be standing...in this day, I will survive all troubles...and in this day, God is still the anchor of my soul!!! The past is behind and today is secure in Him, as long as He is in me and I remain faithful and true in Him. Yesterday is gone, I did learn from it!!! Never to repeat the same. There is joy in my life as I strive to continue this journey with the Lord on my side. I live this life I talk about and pray to be a blessing in the hands of God and in the work of the ministry.

I am a over comer. I live to please God. I heard God speak on the inside of me. I know that He is with me and no weapon that is formed against me shall prosper. The answer is on the inside because God is on the inside. He has given me the courage to wait on the Lord and He shall bring it to pass... Whatever you need, it lies within. Greater is He that is in us, than he that is in the world. Ye are of God, little children, and have overcome them: because greater is he that is in you, than he that is in the world. I John 4:4. Jesus Christ came into this world to save sinners and to seek those that are lost. I was lost and he found me!!!

My revelation in the dream showed me who the people in the dream realistically were. The winds also represented important people in my life that were motivated by evil spirits to do me great harm. The protection and the love of God yet is encamped around about me. My angels fought in my defense and do stand ready to be used at command. The dream prepared the way for some of the troubles I had to face, but the spiritual insight took all fears away. I was given the faith of God to believe that my expected end will be great!!! I have learned first hand of his goodness, and trust in Him alone. If God be for you, who can be against you?

As we come to the end of this literary journey, thank you for participating in reading a soul awakening message that allowed opportunity for you to be revived and encouraged in your spiritual understanding. We can celebrate together that with God all things are possible. We are fresh in our minds to comprehend the demands of the day and strong in our spirit because of the solid Word of God, that will never fail!!! His joy and His goodness has made us glad. There is a now confidence that has come and the faithful promises of God is like money in the bank... according to the power that works in you...Have the faith to believe in the Lord Jesus and always know, it does not matter what you may go through in your life, "THE ANSWER IS ON THE INSIDE!!!"

THE SEED PLANTER CONTINUES

About the Author

She openly conveys her past and the choices that resulted in years of pain because of her mistakes. Rosie L. Rheaves learned the hard way... and now wants to encourage you through God-given abilities how to avoid the pitfalls of life. After accepting Jesus into her life, dramatic changes took place and she soon discovered who she was destined to be.

She has apostolic foundation and lives accordingly to the Holy Scriptures written in the Bible. She is spirit filled and ever increasing in the knowledge of God. Her assignment is to write and make the vision plain... compelling men and women to believe and accept Jesus as both Lord and Savior.

Printed in the United States
29070LVS00003B/193-300